The PALM
IDENTIFIER

AN EASY GUIDE TO CULTIVATING AND
IDENTIFYING OVER 100 SPECIES OF PALMS.

The PALM
IDENTIFIER

AN EASY GUIDE TO CULTIVATING AND
IDENTIFYING OVER 100 SPECIES OF PALMS.

MARTIN GIBBONS

SIMON & SCHUSTER
AUSTRALIA

The Palm Identifier
1997

First published in Australia in 1993 by
Simon & Schuster Australia
20 Barcoo Street, East Roseville, NSW 2069

Reprinted 1995, 1996, 1997

Viacom International
Sydney New York London Toronto Tokyo Singapore

Copyright © 1993 Quintet Publishing Limited
All rights reserved. No part of this publication may be
reproduced, stored in a retrieval system or transmitted in
any form or by any means, electronic, mechanical,
photocopying, recording or otherwise, without the
permission of the publisher in writing.

National Library of Australia
Cataloguing in Publication data

Gibbons, Martin. 1945-.
The Palm Identifier

Includes index
ISBN 0 7318 0083 4

1. Palms. 2. Identification. I. Title

635.97745

This book was designed and produced by
Quintet Publishing Limited
6 Blundell Street
London N7 9BH

Project Editor: Laura Sandelson
Creative Director: Richard Dewing
Designers: Nicky Chapman, Stuart Walden
Editor: Diana Brinton

Typeset in Great Britain by
Central Southern Typesetters, Eastbourne
Manufactured in Singapore by
J. Film Process Singapore Pte Ltd
Printed in Singapore by
Star Standard Industries Pte Ltd

Contents

INTRODUCTION 6

    CULTIVATION 8

    GLOSSARY 12

    HOW TO USE THIS BOOK 13

PALM IDENTIFIER 14

INDEX 80

INTRODUCTION

INTRODUCTION

Palms form an integral and important part of the vegetation of the tropics and sub-tropics, and there are some 3,800 known species. Not all grow either in deserts or on white, sandy beaches, as is popularly supposed. The great majority grow deep in the gloomy rainforest and perhaps never see the sun, certainly not as young plants. It is for this reason that many species can adapt to life as house plants, and some will tolerate even quite deep shade.

Further, there are many species that grow a long way from the tropics, and it comes as a surprise to many people to discover that, far from needing heat and humidity to grow well, a good number of palms actually prefer cool climates, and will thrive outdoor in temperate areas.

Many species of palm are difficult even for the experts to identify, since they differ only in flower or pollen details. However, most of the palms that are more commonly encountered are relatively easy to tell apart, having major, often unique, characteristics which, with guidance, enable amateur and professional plant spotters alike to tell the difference. It is on these species that this book concentrates, and it is hoped that it will prove not only a useful guide, but a means of adding to the enjoyment on any holiday or business trip to the tropics. Each species is illustrated in colour, and the text provides recognition pointers to the main characteristics of the palm – its overall height, origin, leaf shape, trunk size and so on – so that, with these in mind, recognition should be quite easy.

Many people like to grow palms, either in their home or greenhouse, or – if they are lucky enough to live in a warm climate – their garden. It is hoped that this book will prove of practical use to all readers, as both the indoor and outdoor cultivation requirements of each species are discussed.

The International Palm Society is an organization dedicated to those interested in palms, and members receive a quarterly magazine *Principes*, in which they can read and learn about these fascinating plants. The society's address is PO Box 368 Lawrence, Kansas 66044, USA. In Europe, the European Palm Society caters for palm enthusiasts with a specific interest in the more cold-hardy species, and those that prefer temperate conditions. Their colour magazine *Chamaerops*, also a quarterly, can be obtained from the European Palm Society, The Palm Centre, 563 Upper Richmond Road West, London SW14 7ED.

In Australia, the Palm and Cycad Societies of Australia Incorporated, publishes a monthly newsletter and has branches in most capital cities. More information can be obtained by writing to the head office at PO Box 1134 Milton, Queensland 4064, Australia.

CULTIVATION

LEFT The Chameadorea elegans *has been underwatered. It also carries the symptoms of red spider mite — light brown patches on the edges and eventually over the whole of some leaves. Daily mist spraying acts as a preventative, since it keeps up the humidity.*

CULTIVATION
INDOOR PALMS

Many palms that are available as house plants need only the minimum of care and attention to thrive; others are perhaps more difficult, but then again, perhaps more rewarding. Like other houseplants, palms need certain conditions, and these are considered under the following categories – light, temperature, water, humidity, feed.

LIGHT The majority of palms for indoor use require bright, indirect light. Direct sunlight through glass, especially during the summer months, can scorch the leaves of the plant and eventually kill it, though this is not a problem during winter, when your palm should be positioned to take the best advantage of whatever light is available. Plants can either be screened from direct sunlight with nets, blinds or shades, or perhaps be positioned in a window which gets no direct sunlight.

Some palms can tolerate quite low light. These include the Lady palm *(Rhapis excelsa)*, the Pygmy date palm *(Phoenix roebelenii)* and the Fish tail palm *(Caryota mitis)*. It must be admitted, however, that although these plants will put up with low light, they do better in brighter conditions, and it may be advisable to move them to a brighter spot for about one week in every three. Many house palms can be stood outside during the warmer months of the year, when they will benefit from being placed in dappled shade.

TEMPERATURE A palm's requirements as to temperature can be guessed at from its origin. Is it from the tropics? If so, it will almost certainly require warm conditions to thrive, though it is sometimes surprising what cool conditions some tropical palms will put up with, and even thrive in. Is it from desert regions (a date palm, a Brahea, or a Washingtonia, for example)? If so, it will require hot, dry and bright conditions, but will also be able to tolerate very cold temperatures, for short periods. Some palms can put up with temperatures well below freezing, and the hardiest of these (such as Trachycarpus or Chamaerops) make wonderful specimens for the garden, even in temperate zones.

WATER This is without doubt the subject that causes most concern among house plant owners, who are equally terrified of over- and under-watering. The answer is simple; let the surface of the soil dry out slightly, and then give the soil a thorough soak. *Don't* give the palm a little water every day. *Don't* let your palm stand in water, and *don't* let the soil remain waterlogged. *Do* allow the surface of the soil to dry out first. *Do* give a thorough soak to the soil, ideally by immersion if the plant is manageable. If the soil becomes too dry, it will shrink away from the edges of the pot; when water is applied, it will run around the soil instead of through it, and the water appearing in the saucer below may be taken as an indication that the plant has had enough. Not so! Immerse the plant to correct this condition.

HUMIDITY As with light, the origin of the palm can be a guide as to its humidity requirements. Small delicate tropical palms will obviously require a humid atmosphere; plants from the desert will not. Interestingly, palms can be surprisingly adaptable, and new leaves grown in a drier atmosphere will be more tolerant of dry air than those on the same plant which grew in the tropics. Use a hand mister often – as often as you like. Install an electric humidifier which will benefit the plants as well as furniture, paintings, and indeed the human inhabitants. In a glasshouse or conservatory, splash water about liberally in summer; in winter, open the windows to allow fresh, humid air to enter from time to time.

FEED There are now many proprietary brands of house-plant fertilizer on the market, and most of these will be fine for your palms. Spring is the time to begin giving fertilizer to your palms, according to the manufacturer's instructions, perhaps once a week, or once every two weeks, or maybe with every watering. Don't over-fertilize potted palms, as this is one of the causes of browning leaf tips.

ABOVE All palms, like the Kentia *are extremely sensitive to chemicals. Leaves should always be cleaned with a damp sponge, never a chemical cleaner.*

CARYOTA

TRACHYCARPUS

CHAMEADOREA

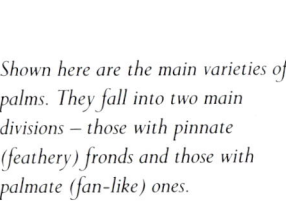

Shown here are the main varieties of palms. They fall into two main divisions – those with pinnate (feathery) fronds and those with palmate (fan-like) ones.

CHRYSALIDOCARPUS

HOWEA

RHAPIS

PHOENIX

LYTOCARYUM

OUTDOOR PALMS

If you have the climate and the space, then growing palms outdoors is the ideal way to enjoy these wonderful plants. What you can grow obviously depends on where you live; those near the equator have a much larger choice, of course, but even in temperate regions such as Britain and the northern United States there are still several possibilities. Even here, the range can be increased if you are prepared to protect your palms in the colder weather.

Consider long and hard before planting your palm in the garden. What goes in as a small seedling, can grow to a huge and overpowering tree in perhaps just a few years. Some palms grow very quickly, especially in the tropics, and can completely dominate a garden in a remarkably short space of time. However, unlike most other trees, their ultimate shape and size is totally predictable. In temperate countries, this problem is less acute, but is still a consideration.

Palms have relatively fine roots, and are not a danger to walls, drains and foundations. They can be planted quite close to walls, from which they will then lean out in characteristic fashion.

Be careful with your choice of palms – many are primadonnas, demanding a central position and lots of attention. Too many of these in a single garden will create confusion and lack of balance. It is preferable to have one or two main subjects, with perhaps a few smaller palms for under-planting. Palms grow well with yuccas, cordylines, bamboos and pines, and a mixed group can look very effective.

PLANTING OUT Your palm will probably go in as a small seedling. Having given due consideration to the above, dig a hole, perhaps putting in some good topsoil, or compost, and position the new arrival. Planting your seedling at the bottom of a saucer-shaped depression will facilitate watering. For the first few years – until well established – most palms will require protection from too much sun, especially in hot climates. This can be achieved in a variety of ways, including shade netting. Dappled sunlight is fine.

Water well for the first few weeks, until active growth is noticed. Thereafter, the plant's requirements will differ according to its original habitat. Generally speaking, well-drained soil, an abundance of water (especially in dry weather) and adequate fertilizing will supply all its needs. Large palms take a lot of fertilizing, and an annual top dressing with stable manure, or well-rotted compost will work wonders.

Your palm may arrive as an established tree, either in rootball form or in a tub. Don't underestimate the weight of a large palm. Any palm with more than a couple of feet of stout trunk will require lifting tackle, or perhaps a small crane, to move it safely. A date palm, for instance, with just a metre of trunk, will weigh close on a ton. Prepare the planting site well in advance, and the palm can be delivered straight to the hole.

Again, water plentifully until new growth is observed; this is an indication that new roots will have formed, and the watering can be eased. However, a newly planted palm, whatever its size, should never be allowed to dry out, and should not be given fertilizer for twelve months.

Garden palms require little in the way of maintenance, just the removal of old dead leaves which, if not shed cleanly by the particular species, need to be trimmed off, with a saw or secateurs.

GLOSSARY

AXIL: the angle between leaf and trunk.

BI-PINNATE: leaf shape unique to the *Caryota* palms (Fish tail), where each leaflet is further divided.

CABBAGE: the undeveloped and unexpanded young leaves of a palm, eaten as a vegetable ("heart of palm") in some countries, and exported to the west as "millionaire's salad" as its collection means the death of the tree.

COSTAPALMATE: a fan-shaped leaf but with the leaf stem extending well into the leaf blade. Almost a half way stage between palmate and pinnate.

CROWNSHAFT: in some palms, the lower end of the petiole is flattened and forms an unbroken tube around the trunk of the tree. When the leaf dies, this splits and falls with the leaf, leaving a scar or ring around the trunk.

HASTULA: the point at which the petiole meets the leaf blade of fan palms, forming a small ridge or crest, on one or both faces of the leaf. In one or two cases only, it is absent.

PALMATE: a leaf that is fan-shaped or hand-shaped.

PETIOLE: the stem or stalk of the leaf.

PINNATE: a leaf with a central stem, with leaflets either side, as in a feather.

HOW TO USE THIS BOOK

This book is laid out so as to give the maximum amount of information in the clearest possible way. The introduction contains general hints and advice on plant care, which is amplified in the identifier section of the book. This deals individually with a wide variety of indoor and outdoor palms. Arranged alphabetically, each entry contains a picture of the palm with its family or genus name and common name, information about its distinguishing characteristics, cultivation habits and an easy care guide. The symbols given below accompany each entry and are intended to give vital information about the size of the palm, the leaf shape and trunk at a glance.

Ideal as an indoor or conservatory plant

SIZE

small	large
medium	massive

LEAF SHAPE

fan	costapalmate
feather	simple (entire)
bipinnate	

TRUNK

solitary	absent
multiple (clustering)	

Palm Identifier

ACOELORRHAPHE WRIGHTII (SYN. *PAUROTIS WRIGHTII*)
SILVER SAW PALMETTO

An unmistakable clumping palm, usually with a few taller trunks dominating the rest, the silver saw palmetto is much used in Florida for street and park decoration.
ORIGIN Central America, West Indies and Florida.
MATURE HEIGHT To 4.5–6m/15–20ft.
TRUNK Multiple, slender, covered with brown fibre.
LEAF Fan shaped, with silver back.
FLOWER STALK From among the leaves.
FRUIT Small and round, black when ripe.
SEED Small, round.
CULTIVATION The seeds germinate rapidly and easily. *OUTDOORS* A palm for the tropics and sub-tropics it is widely cultivated. It prefers damp soil, or at least access to permanent underground moisture. *INDOORS* Little is known about its use as an indoor plant.

AIPHANES EROSA
MACAW PALM

An interesting palm, it is covered in sharp spines from an early age, which should be taken into account when choosing an outdoor site.
ORIGIN West Indies.
MATURE HEIGHT To 4.5m/15ft.
TRUNK Slim, solitary, dark, covered in fine sharp black spines.
LEAF Pinnate, with long leaflets, held flat, the petiole and, to an extent, the underparts of the leaf, are also spiny.
FLOWER STALK From among the leaf bases; fragrant, creamy flowers.
FRUIT Red when ripe.
SEED Small and round, distinctively pitted on the surface.
CULTIVATION The seeds germinate easily if fresh. *OUTDOORS* The Macaw palm is an attractive small tree for the tropics and sub-tropics. *INDOORS* Certainly suitable for a moist conservatory, it would make an interesting addition to any collection.

ARCHONTOPHOENIX ALEXANDRAE
ALEXANDER PALM, KING PALM

A beautiful, easily cultivated and popular palm, the Alexander or king palm is commonly seen in the tropics and sub-tropics.
ORIGIN Eastern Australia.
MATURE HEIGHT To 18m/60ft.
TRUNK Solitary, light grey, covered with old leaf scars, often swollen at the base; mid-green crownshaft.
LEAF Pinnate, held flat, sometimes twisted so it is perpendicular to the ground; the underside of the leaflet is silvery — a key identification factor.
FLOWER STALK From below the crownshaft, cream colour.
FRUIT Round, 18mm/¾in in diameter, red when ripe. Borne in huge numbers.
SEED Covered in longitudinal fibres.
CULTIVATION The seeds germinate within a few weeks, and subsequent seedling growth is also fast. *OUTDOORS* Fast growing, the king palm is cultivated in tropics and sub-tropics. *INDOORS* This may be cultivated indoors, but requires high levels of light and humidity.

ARCHONTOPHOENIX CUNNINGHAMIANA
BANGALOW PALM

A common and popular, slender pinnate palm, it is similar to *A. alexandrae* in appearance.
ORIGIN Eastern Australia.
MATURE HEIGHT To 18m or 21m/60ft or 70ft.
TRUNK Slim, grey, with old leaf scars, mid-green crownshaft.
LEAF Pinnate, mid-green, but without the silvery undersides of *A. alexandrae*.
FLOWER STALK From below the the crownshaft, violet colour.
FRUIT Small, red when ripe, and borne in huge numbers.
SEED Covered in longitudinal fibres.
CULTIVATION The fibrous seeds germinate easily and quickly.
OUTDOORS An easy outdoor palm for tropics, sub-tropics and warm temperate climates, it shows some tolerance to cold and will take a few degrees of frost. It is also fast growing. *INDOORS* The bangalow palm requires good light and humidity, but can be grown indoors.

PALM IDENTIFIER

*A*RECA CATECHU
BETEL NUT PALM

A familiar and attractive palm in the tropics, it is commonly grown for its seed, – the betel nut, which is a mild narcotic.
ORIGIN South-East Asia.
MATURE HEIGHT To 15m/50ft.
TRUNK Solitary, distinctly ringed, with crownshaft.
LEAF Broad leaflets, or sometimes broad and narrow on the same leaf, the tips being jagged.
FLOWER STALK From below the crownshaft.
FRUIT Red when ripe, to 5cm/2in long.
SEED Oval, but flattened at one end, it is chewed, in tropical countries, with other ingredients, as a mild stimulant.
CULTIVATION The large seeds germinate quickly if fresh, and subsequent growth is also fast. *OUTDOORS* An excellent palm for the tropics and sub-tropics, it prefers a shady location, and plenty of water. *INDOORS* The betel nut palm requires warmth and humidity, but may successfully be cultivated indoors. Plants are sometimes sold in garden centres as "Mini Cocos".

*A*RECA IPOT

Although not dissimilar to *A. catechu,* it is smaller and daintier.
ORIGIN The Philippines.
MATURE HEIGHT To 3.5m or 4.5m/12ft or 15ft.
TRUNK Solitary, distinctly ringed, with swollen crownshaft.
LEAF A mixture of wide and narrow leaflets on the one leaf; the ends of the leaflets look as though chewed by some animal.
FLOWER STALK From below the crownshaft.
FRUIT Red when ripe, to 5cm/2in long.
SEED Oval, but flattened at one end.
CULTIVATION The large seeds germinate quickly if fresh, and subsequent growth is fast. *OUTDOORS* An excellent palm for the tropics and sub-tropics, it prefers a shady location, with an abundance of water in dry weather. *INDOORS* If warmth and humidity can be provided, it may be successfully grown indoors.

ARECA TRIANDRA

An attractive clumping palm for the moist tropics, where it is commonly grown.
ORIGIN Malaysia and India.
MATURE HEIGHT To 4.5m/15ft.
TRUNK Multiple, distinctly ringed, with crownshafts.
LEAF Wide and narrow leaflets are often found on the same leaf, the tips being jagged.
FLOWER STALK From below the crownshaft.
FRUIT Orange/red when ripe, to 2.5cm/1in long.
SEED Oval, but flattened at one end.
CULTIVATION The large seeds germinate quickly if fresh, and subsequent growth is fast. *OUTDOORS* Another excellent palm for the tropics and sub-tropics, it prefers a position out of direct sunlight, and plenty of water. *INDOORS A. triandra* requires warmth and humidity, but indoor cultivation may be successful.

ARECA VESTIARIA

An attractive small-to-medium palm, it is most notable for its orange crownshaft, a feature which easily distinguishes it from all other arecas, and most other palms.
ORIGIN Indonesia.
MATURE HEIGHT To 9m/30ft.
TRUNK Solitary, slim, sometimes seen with stilt roots; it has a crownshaft, which is bright orange in colour.
LEAF Typical areca feather-shaped leaf.
FLOWER STALK From below the crownshaft.
FRUIT Orange in colour when ripe, 2.5cm/1in long.
SEED Oval, flattened at one end.
CULTIVATION This is easily grown from seed, which germinates readily, and plants can be quite fast growing. *OUTDOORS* A palm for the tropics and sub-tropics, *A. vestiaria* is an excellent addition to any collection. *INDOORS* It is not known to have been tried indoors.

A R E N G A   E N G L E R I

This attractive small palm grows well in climates ranging from tropical to temperate, and will even take some frost.
ORIGIN Taiwan.
MATURE HEIGHT To 3m/10ft.
TRUNK Multiple, short, covered with old leaf fibres.
LEAF The long, broad, pinnate leaf is green above, silvery below; there are long, narrow leaflets, often with irregular edges and tips.
FLOWER STALK From among the leaves; that particular stem dying after fruiting.
FRUIT Round, 12mm/½in in diameter, dark red when ripe. The pulp is caustic and should not be handled without gloves.
SEED There are two or three per fruit, with corresponding flat sides.
CULTIVATION The seeds are erratic to germinate, some sprouting within a few weeks, others taking months. *OUTDOORS* Plants grow slowly to a broad, bushy shape, much wider than tall. This palm is cold tolerant, so worth a try in cooler climates, where it is very slow growing. It can be planted in either sun or shade. *INDOORS* This has not been tested for indoor use, and is probably not suitable.

A R E N G A   P I N N A T A
SUGAR PALM

This large, towering, untidy palm is cultivated for its sugary sap.
ORIGIN South-East Asia.
MATURE HEIGHT To 18m/60ft or more.
TRUNK Solitary, 30cm/12in in diameter, covered with old leaf bases and black dusty fibres, with spines 7.5cm/3in or 10cm/4in long.
LEAF Long, pinnate, erect, with long narrow leaflets, dark green above, silvery beneath.
FLOWER STALK When the tree has reached maturity, the first inflorescence appears in the highest leaf axil, subsequent flower stalks appearing lower and lower down the tree. When the final one has produced flowers and seeds, the tree dies.
FRUIT Round, dark red to purple, 4cm/1½in in diameter; the fruit pulp should not be handled.
SEED Usually three per fruit, flat sided to fit.
CULTIVATION Sugar palms are easily grown from seed, which germinates quickly. *OUTDOORS* Fast growing in the tropics, they are slower in cooler areas and are not ideal for decorative purposes, firstly because of the stinging crystals in the fruit, and secondly because of the tree's moderately short life. *INDOORS* Warmth and humidity are required for this fast-growing palm.

ARENGA UNDULATIFOLIA

A hugely broad, clumping palm. Very attractive, and requiring plenty of room to show it off adequately.
ORIGIN Borneo.
MATURE HEIGHT To 9m/30ft, but usually much broader than tall.
TRUNK Multiple, messy, impenetrable, covered with old leaf fibres, usually hidden by the huge leaves.
LEAF Very long and wide pinnate leaf, it is similar to A. *pinnata,* but its distinctive and attractive wavy edges are unmistakable.
FLOWER STALK Growing among the leaves, as the other *Arenga* species.
FRUIT Round, a dark purplish red when ripe – handle with care!
SEED Usually three per fruit, with round backs and flattened faces to fit together.
CULTIVATION The seeds germinate quickly and easily if fresh.
OUTDOORS This is a beautiful and fast-growing palm for the tropics.
INDOORS Not much is known about its requirements inside, but these are likely to be satisfied by high humidity and warmth.

BACTRIS GASIPAES
PEACH PALM

A very spiny palm, this is grown commercially for its sweet fruit, often to be seen in the markets of its native countries.
ORIGIN Central and South America.
MATURE HEIGHT To 9m/30ft.
TRUNK Clustering, slim, densely covered in black spines.
LEAF Pinnate, mid-green, with very spiny leafstalks.
FLOWER STALK From among the leaves.
FRUIT Yellow, the size and shape of a peach, grown as food in tropical countries.
SEED Round, 18mm/¾in in diameter, and very hard; sometimes missing from cultivated plants.
CULTIVATION Eating the fruit and planting the seed is twice the fun, and the latter germinate quite quickly. *OUTDOORS* Tropical conditions are required, with an abundance of water. Plants are quite fast growing in favourable conditions. *INDOORS* This species is not known to have been tried indoors.

*B*ISMARCKIA NOBILIS
BISMARCK PALM

A huge and attractive tropical fan palm, it is one of many unusual species which come from this interesting island.
ORIGIN Madagascar.
MATURE HEIGHT To 45–60m/150–200ft.
TRUNK Stout, grey, smooth.
LEAF Huge fan leaf, up to 3m/10ft across, blue grey in colour.
FLOWER STALK From among the leaves.
FRUIT Round, 4cm/1½in in diameter.
SEED The size and shape of a walnut.
CULTIVATION The seeds germinate without any problems, usually within two to three months of sowing. The first leaves already have the distinctive colour of the older tree. *OUTDOORS* A beautiful palm for the drier tropics. *INDOORS* Nothing is known of its cultural requirements indoors.

*B*ORASSODENDRON MACHADONIS

This large fan palm makes an attractive plant for the tropical garden.
ORIGIN Malaysia, where it is rare.
MATURE HEIGHT To 30m/100ft or more.
TRUNK Stout, grey, covered in closely arranged old leaf scars.
LEAF Fan shaped, with characteristic deep splits between the broad segments.
FLOWER STALK From among the leaves.
FRUIT Large, round, 10–12.5cm/4–5in in diameter, glossy dark red brown.
SEED Usually 2 per fruit, 7.5cm/3in long, round on one side, flat on the other, covered in persistent, straw-coloured, parallel fibres.
CULTIVATION The large seeds either germinate very quickly, or not at all; freshness would probably be the determining factor. *OUTDOORS* Tropical or subtropical conditions are required, together with a good water supply. *INDOORS* This has not been tried as a house plant.

BORASSUS FLABELLIFER

After the coconut, this is arguably the most numerous and widespread palm in the world, and in its native India and Malaysia there are huge stands covering thousands of acres. A sugary sap is obtained by cutting off the unopened inflorescence, up to a gallon of sap being collected in this way in a single day. It is a labour-intensive process; the natives climb up each tree in turn, by means of a strap around their waist and the trunk, and using the old leaf bases as footholds. The sap is then reduced, either by boiling, to form a crude sugar, or by fermenting, to produce "toddy", which is an alcoholic liquor.

As well as this, the tree has literally hundreds of other uses. The timber is very hard and black, and is much used in construction. The big leaves are used in thatching and for paper, and the first long taproot produced by the seed is a much sought-after vegetable delicacy.

BORASSUS FLABELLIFER
PALMYRA PALM

Very widely grown in the tropics, it is perhaps the most numerous palm in the world.
ORIGIN India and Malaysia.
MATURE HEIGHT To 36m/120ft.
TRUNK Thick, very hard, black and smooth.
LEAF Palmate, to 3m/10ft across, forming a distinctive spherical crown.
FLOWER STALK From among the leaves.
FRUIT Very large, to 15cm/6in in diameter, shiny dark brown in colour.
SEED One to three per fruit. Large, covered in light brown, wavy fibres like coarse fur.
CULTIVATION The seed produces a taproot 60–90cm/2–3ft long before any top growth appears, so it should be planted either in a deep container, or in its permanent position in the ground. *OUTDOORS* This large palm is suitable for the dry tropics. *INDOORS* It is unsuitable for use indoors.

BRAHEA ARMATA
MEXICAN BLUE PALM

In moonlight, the blue leaves of this beautiful and cold-hardy palm look almost white.
ORIGIN Southern California.
MATURE HEIGHT To 12m/40ft.
TRUNK Solitary, thick and grey, either with persistent dead leaves, or smooth and covered with old leaf scars.
LEAF Stiff, palmate, covered with a pale blue bloom; looks its best in hot, bright and dry conditions.
FLOWER STALK From among the leaves, and arching out far beyond them.
FRUIT 12mm/½in in diameter, brown.
SEED Round.
CULTIVATION Germination is erratic, the seeds sometimes sprouting in a few weeks, sometimes taking a year or more. *OUTDOORS* This palm will grow in climates ranging from sub-tropical to temperate. It requires full sun, well drained soil, and an adequate supply of water. Slow growing, especially in cooler areas, it has the advantage of being somewhat frost tolerant. *INDOORS* The Mexican blue palm is probably not suitable for indoor cultivation because of its high light requirements, but it would tolerate dry air well and is a wonderful plant for the glasshouse or conservatory.

BRAHEA EDULIS
GUADALOUPE PALM

An attractive and fast-growing fan palm for temperate to sub-tropical regions.
ORIGIN Guadaloupe Island, off the Mexican coast.
MATURE HEIGHT To 15m/50ft.
TRUNK Stout; old leaves self-prune, leaving leaf scars.
LEAF Mid-green, palmate, stiffly held.
FLOWER STALK From among the leaves.
FRUIT Hanging down in bunches, the fruits are dark brown to black, 2.5cm/1in in diameter, with an edible, though thin, sweet pulp.
SEED 18mm/¾in in diameter.
CULTIVATION The round seeds germinate more easily than those of *B. armata*, but germination still tends to be erratic. *OUTDOORS* This will grow outdoors from the sub-tropics to temperate zones, where it will stand some frost. Faster growing than *B. armata*, it requires full sun, well-drained, rich soil, and an abundance of water. *INDOORS* Its high light requirements make it generally unsuitable for a house plant, but if this need can be fulfilled it would be worth a try.

Butia capitata
BUTIA PALM, JELLY PALM

A popular and attractive palm for a wide range of climates, it is sometimes grown for the edible fruit, from which jam or jelly is made. This is one of the few hardy feather palms.
ORIGIN Brazil.
MATURE HEIGHT To 7.5m/25ft.
TRUNK Grey, stout and smooth, but with old leaf scars.
LEAF Unmistakable – pinnate, strongly recurved, blue green in colour.
FLOWER STALK From among the lower leaves.
FRUIT 2.5cm/1in long, oval, yellow to red, with a sweet pulp.
SEED 18mm/³⁄₄in long, oval with three germination pores at one end.
CULTIVATION Seeds are erratic to germinate, and can take from a few weeks to a year or more. *OUTDOORS* The jelly palm grows in a wide range of climates, from sub tropics to temperate regions, where it can withstand severe frosts. It prefers full sun and a well-drained soil, with plenty of water. *INDOORS* Its light requirements are probably too high for indoor cultivation, but if you have a very light area it would be worth a try.

Caryota mitis
FISH-TAIL PALM

An interesting and easily cultivated palm, it is commonly grown in the tropics, and readily available as a house plant.
ORIGIN South-East Asia.
MATURE HEIGHT To 7.5 or 9m/25 or 30ft.
TRUNK Multiple, slender.
LEAF Bipinnate, leaflets triangular, with a ragged edge and a distinctive "fish-tail" shape.
FLOWER STALK Flowers appear from the highest leaf axil first, then progressively downward; when the last one has flowered and fruited, that stem dies, to be replaced by others in the clump.
FRUIT Round, 18mm/³⁄₄in in diameter, dull red when ripe; contains stinging crystals in the pulp, and should be handled with care.
SEED Round or hemispherical, with folds or grooves; dull grey in colour.
CULTIVATION The distinctive seeds germinate easily and quickly if fresh. *OUTDOORS* Easily grown in the tropics, it is slower in the sub-tropics, though it may also be tried in warm temperate areas. Rich soil and an abundance of water are appreciated. *INDOORS* A good indoor palm, it tolerates low to medium light, but prefers bright indirect light, and humidity. Yellowing of the leaves may be caused by lack of iron.

CALAMUS

The palm genus with the largest number of species is *Calamus*, which contains nearly 400 members. It has a wide distribution, ranging from Africa to India and much of South-East Asia, right down to Australia. The slim and flexible trunks, which snake up into the tree tops, are the source of rattan, much used in the manufacture of cane furniture. Although proper management of the industry is now becoming more and more widespread, many species are still considered to be endangered because of over-exploitation. Some methods of collection are very wasteful: sometimes elephants are used to drag the long canes down from the treetops. If one should break, then perhaps hundreds of feet are left suspended, inaccessible, and wasted. The Australian common name, "Wait-a-while", derives from the fact that to escape from entanglement in a *Calamus* clump can be a slow, not to mention a painful, experience.

CALAMUS AUSTRALIS
LAWYER'S CANE

Lawyer's cane is one of a huge family (containing almost 400 species) of spiny, mainly climbing palms from the tropics. The cleaned trunks, known as "Rattan", are used extensively in the manufacture of furniture.
ORIGIN North-eastern Australia.
MATURE HEIGHT Climbs up into the treetops, using other vegetation as a support.
TRUNK Multiple, very slender, sinuous, and covered with sharp spines.
LEAF Pinnate, pretty, with many regular, narrow leaflets; the leafstalk is covered with backward-pointing spines or hooks to aid its climbing habit, and the leaf may bear a long extension (up to 3m/10ft long), similarly armed.
FLOWER STALK Long, pendulous, spiny.
FRUIT Pea-sized, a pale whitish green, covered with scales.
SEED Small, irregularly shaped.
CULTIVATION The small seeds must be absolutely fresh if they are to germinate, which they will do in a few weeks.
OUTDOORS This can be grown in a tropical garden, where it should prove an interesting addition. *INDOORS* Young plants are extremely pretty. They should tolerate low light, but would be more fussy about humidity.

CARYOTA NO

A stunningly beautiful fish-tail palm, with an incredibly complex leaf structure, this is one of the larger caryotas.
ORIGIN Mountainous districts of Borneo and peninsular Malaysia.
MATURE HEIGHT To 21m/70ft.
TRUNK Thick, to 0.6m/2ft in diameter, somewhat swollen towards the middle; light grey in colour, with old leaf scars every foot or so, indicating the speed at which it grows.
LEAF Bipinnate, huge, and held flat; wonderful when viewed from below, in silhouette, leaflets are triangular, with ragged edges.
FLOWER STALK From the highest leaf axil first, then progressively downward; when the last one has flowered and fruited, the tree dies.
FRUIT 4cm/1½in in diameter, almost black when ripe, with caustic crystals in the pulp.
SEED One or two seeds per fruit, consequently round or half round in shape.
CULTIVATION The seeds germinate easily and quickly, if fresh.
OUTDOORS This caryota is sub-tropical to tropical in its requirements.
INDOORS A good indoor palm, it will tolerate low to medium light, but prefers bright indirect light, and humidity. Yellowing of the leaves may be caused by lack of iron.

CARYOTA OBTUSA
FISH-TAIL PALM

The largest of the fish-tail palms, it is an awesome sight.
ORIGIN Northern India, China.
MATURE HEIGHT To 24 or 27m/80 or 90ft.
TRUNK Massive, light grey, with old leaf scars.
LEAF Huge, bipinnate and flatly held.
FLOWER STALK From the highest leaf axil first, then progressively downward; when the last one has flowered and fruited, the tree dies.
FRUIT 4cm/1½in in diameter, dull red when ripe.
SEED One to three per fruit, shaped accordingly.
CULTIVATION The seeds germinate without difficulty. *OUTDOORS* Suitable for the tropics, sub-tropics and warm temperate regions, this is a hungry and thirsty palm. *INDOORS* Little is known of its requirements indoors, but these are likely to be the same as for the other fish-tail palms.

CARYOTA URENS
WINE OR JAGGERY PALM

Both an alcoholic liquor and sugar are made from the sap.
ORIGIN India, Burma, Sri Lanka.
MATURE HEIGHT To 18m/60ft.
TRUNK Solitary, grey with old leaf scars as rings every 30cm/12in or so, one for every old leaf.
LEAF Not held flat, but tumbling, arching and pendulous, leaflets are the usual fish-tail shape, but are generally of a darker colour than those of other species.
FLOWER STALK From the highest leaf axil first, then progressively downward; when the last one has flowered and fruited, the tree dies.
FRUIT 18mm/¾in circumference, dark red when ripe.
SEED One or two per fruit, thus round or half round, as with other caryotas, the fruit contains caustic crystals.
CULTIVATION Fresh seeds germinate easily and within a few weeks. *OUTDOORS* The wine palm can be grown in zones ranging from tropical to warm temperate. Rich soil, and an abundance of both water and fertilizer are required for optimum growth. *INDOORS* A good indoor palm, it will tolerate low to medium light, but prefers bright indirect light, and humidity. Yellowing of the leaves may be caused by lack of iron.

CEROXYLON ALPINUM (SYN. C. ANDICOLA)
ANDEAN WAX PALM

This beautiful palm comes from the high Andes mountains of South America. The genus contains some of the tallest known plants, and the wax from the trunks is used commercially.
ORIGIN Colombia.
MATURE HEIGHT To 30m/100ft.
TRUNK Solitary, slim, grey, covered with a layer of wax.
LEAF Pinnate, green above, silvery white beneath.
FLOWER STALK From among the leaf bases.
FRUIT 18mm/¾in in diameter, orange red when ripe, with a rough surface.
SEED 12mm/½in in diameter, round and very hard.
CULTIVATION The seeds germinate readily if very fresh; they lose their viability very quickly. Young plants seem to rot away quite easily and should be sprayed with fungicide immediately on germination and perhaps weekly thereafter until established. *OUTDOORS* An exciting palm for temperate and warm temperate areas, it is not suitable for the tropics. Plants will take some frost. *INDOORS* Nothing is known of its requirements as an indoor plant.

CEROXYLON QUINDIUENSE
ANDEAN WAX PALM

Similar to *C. alpinum* in many respects, but grows at a higher elevation, and is taller.
ORIGIN Colombia.
MATURE HEIGHT To an incredible 60m/200ft.
TRUNK Smooth, grey, covered with a thin coating of wax.
LEAF Pinnate, green above, yellowish grey beneath.
FLOWER STALK From among the leaf bases.
FRUIT 18mm/³⁄₄in in diameter, orange red when ripe, with a smooth surface.
SEED 12mm/¹⁄₂in in diameter and very hard.
CULTIVATION The seeds germinate readily if very fresh; they speedily lose their viability. Young plants seem prone to rot; they should be sprayed with fungicide immediately on germination, and regularly thereafter until well established. *OUTDOORS* An exciting palm for temperate and warm temperate areas, and tolerant of frost to some extent, it is not suitable for the tropics. *INDOORS* Nothing is known of its requirements as an indoor plant.

CHAMAEROPS HUMILIS
MEDITERRANEAN FAN PALM

An extremely variable palm, it is commonly grown for cooler regions.
ORIGIN Western Mediterranean countries.
MATURE HEIGHT Cultivated plants can grow to 6m/20ft, wild specimens rarely more than 90cm–1.2m/3–4ft.
TRUNK Clumping, multiple, about 10–12.5cm/4–5in in diameter, in cultivation often forming a large bush; trunks are covered with old leaf bases.
LEAF Fan shaped, green, 60–90cm/2–3ft in diameter, very stiff leaflets; petiole armed with sharp spines; sometimes silver or blue forms are seen.
FLOWER STALK From among leaves.
FRUIT Round to oval, red brown when ripe, and 2.5cm/1in long.
SEED Oval, fibrous, 18mm/³⁄₄in.
CULTIVATION The seeds germinate in about six weeks. *OUTDOORS* Suitable for most climatic zones, this hardy palm is very cold tolerant, surviving temperatures perhaps as low as −10°C/14°F. *INDOORS* It requires bright light to succeed, and is therefore not entirely suitable as a house plant, but it is an excellent conservatory plant.

CHAMEADOREA ELEGANS

The humble parlour palm, one of the most popular house palms in the world, comes from the rainforests of Mexico. Because of its tolerance of poor light, dry air, drought, flood and general neglect, it makes a very easy house plant. Additionally, seeds are produced when the palm is just two or three years old; germination is fast and reliable, and subsequent seedling growth is also speedy. All these advantages make this species a very attractive proposition for the nurseryman; parlour palms are grown by the million in Europe and America for the house plant trade. It is perfectly possible for parlour palms to produce seed at home, but as the sexes are on separate plants, two or more plants are required, and an even greater number increases the chances of successful pollination. When the tiny yellow flowers open, use a soft paintbrush to transfer pollen from one plant to another. Do this several times a day while the flowers are open. If you have been successful in aiding Mother Nature, the seeds will begin to develop within a few weeks – green at first, then black when ripe. When the first seed falls, the rest can be removed, dried and cleaned, and then planted to begin the process again.

CHAMEADOREA ELEGANS
PARLOUR PALM

One of a large genus of some 100 species, this is so well known that it hardly needs any description. Tolerant of low light, and general abuse. It is very easily grown.
ORIGIN Mexico.
MATURE HEIGHT To 1.8–2.1m/6–7ft.
TRUNK Slim, solitary, dark green, distinctly ringed with old leaf scars.
LEAF Dark green, pinnate.
FLOWER STALK From the lowest leaf axils.
FRUIT Small, round, black when ripe.
SEED Small, round.
CULTIVATION The parlour palm is easily grown from fresh seed. *OUTDOORS* It grows best in a shady position, with access to a steady supply of water, and will succeed in climates ranging from tropical to temperate. *INDOORS* Excellent as a house plant, living for a good number of years, it will stand low to medium light, and some cold.

CHAMEADOREA ERUMPENS
BAMBOO PALM

A beautiful and robust-growing palm, it is ideal as a house plant, as it tolerates low light and some cold.
ORIGIN Mexico.
MATURE HEIGHT To 3m/10ft.
TRUNK Slim, multiple, dark green with prominent rings, like bamboo.
LEAF Dark green, pinnate, with fairly broad leaflets.
FLOWER STALK From the lowest leaf axils.
FRUIT Orange in colour, and pea sized.
SEED Small, round.
CULTIVATION The small seeds germinate easily if fresh. *OUTDOORS* Bamboo palms grow best in shade, as sun may burn the leaves. They form an attractive clump in a number of years. *INDOORS* A wonderful house plant, it will tolerate low light and cool conditions, and is fast growing.

CHAMEADOREA GEONOMAEFORMIS

A small palm, with beautiful large leaves, it is not commonly available, but is worth seeking out, either for the home or for a garden in a warm area.
ORIGIN Mexico, Honduras.
MATURE HEIGHT Grows slowly to only 90cm or 1.2m/3 or 4ft.
TRUNK Slim, solitary, dark green, with old leaf scars as rings.
LEAF Large, simple, split into two halves.
FLOWER STALK From the lowest leaf axils.
FRUIT Black when ripe.
SEED Small, round.
CULTIVATION Seeds should be fresh to germinate well. *OUTDOORS* Plant in the warm garden in a shady spot, out of direct sunlight, which can burn the leaves. *INDOORS* This is another excellent indoor palm for position offering low to medium light.

C H A M E A D O R E A
K L O T Z S C H I A N A

This is unusual in its leaf arrangement, which is unique in the palm world.
ORIGIN Mexico.
MATURE HEIGHT To 1.8m/6ft.
TRUNK Solitary, slim, mid-green, with rings left by old leaves.
LEAF Pinnate, with leaflets arranged in irregular groups along the leaf stem.
FLOWER STALK From the lowest leaf axils.
FRUIT Black when ripe.
SEED Small, round.
CULTIVATION Rarely available, the seeds germinate readily if fresh. *OUTDOORS* As with other *Chameadoreas*, choose a shady spot, ideally in the tropical or subtropical garden. *INDOORS* Not much is known of its requirements, but these are likely to be the same as for other members of the genus.

C H A M E A D O R E A   M E T A L L I C A

The unique quality of this species lies in the coloration of the leaves, which have a metallic sheen.
ORIGIN Mexico.
MATURE HEIGHT To only 90cm or 1.2m/3 or 4ft.
TRUNK Slim and dark green in colour, with old leaf rings.
LEAF Simple, divided only at the tip, can range from dark green to almost black in colour, with a unique metallic sheen.
FLOWER STALK From the lowest leaf axils, orange in colour.
FRUIT Black when ripe.
SEED Small, oval.
CULTIVATION Fresh seeds germinate readily. *OUTDOORS* Shade is required if the leaves are to be a good, dark colour. *INDOORS* A perfect indoor palm, it is elegant and attractive, very tolerant of low light, and should be more widely used.

CHAMEADOREA STOLONIFERA

An excellent house plant, it is grown for its attractively bushy shape.
ORIGIN Mexico.
MATURE HEIGHT To 1.8m/6ft.
TRUNK Multiple, very slender, mid-green, each with leaf scars from fallen leaves; the slim stems run along the ground before turning upwards.
LEAF Simple, divided at the tip, mid-green.
FLOWER STALK From the lowest leaf axils.
FRUIT Black when ripe, oval.
SEED Small, oval.
CULTIVATION As with the other members of the genus, the small seeds should be fresh to ensure successful germination. *OUTDOORS* This species will perhaps take more sun than the others, but it still prefers a shady location, in a frost-free garden. *INDOORS* A wonderful house plant, it will tolerate low to medium light.

CHUNIOPHOENIX HAINANENSIS

A beautiful but rare palm, it is related to rhapis.
ORIGIN Hainan Island, China.
MATURE HEIGHT To 6m/20ft.
TRUNK Slim, multiple.
LEAF Much like a very large *Rhapis* leaf, but with no hastula, a feature which distinguishes it from almost every other palm.
FLOWER STALK From among the leaves.
FRUIT Round, bright red when ripe, 2.5cm/1in in diameter.
SEED Round.
CULTIVATION Fresh seeds germinate well, and quickly, and subsequent seedling growth is also quite fast. *OUTDOORS* A warm temperate climate preferred, with high rainfall – frost tolerance is probably minimal. *INDOORS* It has not been used in this way, but should be a good house plant.

CHRYSALIDOCARPUS LUTESCENS
BUTTERFLY PALM; ARECA PALM; GOLDEN CANE PALM

This is probably the most widely-sold palm in the world.
ORIGIN Madagascar.
MATURE HEIGHT To 9m/30ft, but usually seen as a pot plant.
TRUNK Multiple, slim, ringed, sometimes branching just above ground level.
LEAF Yellow petiole if sun-grown, otherwise green; leaf elegant, pale green feather shaped.
FLOWER STALK From below the crownshaft.
FRUIT 18mm/³⁄₄in, oval.
SEED Oval, beaked at one end, dark red or brown.
CULTIVATION The butterfly palm is easily grown in warm temperate to tropical climates, fresh seeds germinating easily and quickly.
OUTDOORS This fast-growing, clumping palm will take either full sun or partial shade, and requires good drainage with lots of water.
INDOORS Perhaps the most popular house palm, it should have bright, indirect light, and does not like the cold.

CHRYSALIDOCARPUS MADAGASCARIENSIS

An attractive relative of *C. lutescens,* it is rarely seen outside botanic gardens.
ORIGIN Madagascar.
MATURE HEIGHT To 6 or 9m/20 or 30ft.
TRUNK Solitary or multiple, 15cm/6in or more in diameter, grey and closely ringed with old leaf scars.
LEAF Plumose (leaflets are on different planes).
FLOWER STALK From below the crownshaft.
FRUIT Similar to *C. lutescens,* but a little smaller.
SEED 12mm/¹⁄₂in, beaked.
CULTIVATION This palm is easily grown from fresh seed. *OUTDOORS* A warm temperate to tropical climate is required, with full sun and ample moisture. *INDOORS* Not much tried, it probably requires bright indirect light.

COCCOTHRINAX ARGENTEA
FLORIDA SILVER PALM

This is a palm of bright sunshine, and dry, alkaline soils.
ORIGIN Southern Florida.
MATURE HEIGHT To 6m/20ft.
TRUNK Solitary, slim, covered with woven fibres.
LEAF A small palmate leaf with distinctive silver undersides.
FLOWER STALK From among leaves.
FRUIT Small, round, brown when ripe.
SEED Tiny, round, wrinkled.
CULTIVATION Seeds germinate within a few weeks or months, but subsequent seedling growth is desperately slow, with one or two grass-like leaves per year. *OUTDOORS* The Florida silver palm requires bright sunshine in a tropical situation; it is well suited to coastal areas. *INDOORS* Not much tried indoors, it would undoubtedly have high light requirements.

COCCOTHRINAX CRINITA

An attractive small palm, it is well-known for the long, pale brown, hair-like fibres that cover the trunk.
ORIGIN Cuba.
MATURE HEIGHT To 6m/20ft, perhaps more.
TRUNK Unmistakable, being completely covered in thick, long hair.
LEAF Fan shaped, regularly cut.
FLOWER STALK From among the leaves.
FRUIT Small and round.
SEED Tiny, round, wrinkled.
CULTIVATION See notes under *C. argentea*.

COCOS NUCIFERA

"Nucifera" means "nut bearing", and "Cocos" comes from the Portuguese word for monkey, an allusion to the three pores or eyes of a coconut which are said to resemble a monkey's face. One of the world's most useful plants, the coconut palm has hundreds of uses and is the staple diet of many people in the tropics. Apart from the obvious use of the flesh (or "endosperm") as food, the coconut water with which the nut is filled provides a refreshing drink. However, the most important use of this intensively farmed tree is the dried flesh, or "copra", which is exported by the millions of tons, and is used in the production of commercial oils.

Wild palms do not produce coconuts until they are many years old, and are very tall, but thanks to science, cultivated forms are mature when only four or five years old, with just a few feet of trunk. The large nuts can thus easily be gathered. It is as a symbol of all things tropical that the coconut palm is best known, and pictures of it are used to promote everything from holidays to shampoo, and from sunbeds to sports cars.

COCOS NUCIFERA
COCONUT PALM

Probably the best known palm in the world, it is used in a thousand ways to represent the tropics, its elegant, often leaning trunks standing as a symbol of tropical holidays.
ORIGIN Not known for sure, but probably the Pacific basin.
MATURE HEIGHT To 30m/100ft, cultivars much less.
TRUNK Characteristic, often leaning, slim, solitary, ringed.
LEAF Feather shaped, regular, green yellow in colour.
FLOWER STALK From among the lower leaves.
FRUIT Oval, large to very large; yellow or green at first, then dry and brown when ripe.
SEED The well-known coconut.
CULTIVATION The large seeds take several months to germinate, and must be planted with the husk entire.
OUTDOORS This is a palm for the humid tropics; various cultivars are available, some of which fruit in only a few years, and when comparatively small. *INDOORS* Although it is often sold as a house plant, its requirements of high humidity, high temperature and high light, make it quite unsuitable. Most plants sold as house plants die within a few weeks or months.

COPERNICIA BAILEYANA
BAILEY'S COPERNICIA PALM

One of a diverse group of 25 species from Cuba and South America, many of which are beautiful, and a few of which are stunning. Grown for the wax that covers the leaves of some species, they also make striking ornamental palms for the tropics and sub-tropics.
ORIGIN Cuba.
MATURE HEIGHT To 15m/50ft.
TRUNK Solitary, thick, smooth.
LEAF Large, stiff fan-shaped leaves covered with a thin layer of wax.
FLOWER STALK From among the leaf bases.
FRUIT Oval, 2.5cm/1in long, brown when ripe.
SEED Small, round, with a few wrinkles.
CULTIVATION The small seeds germinate easily enough, although they may take a few months. However, subsequent seedling growth is very slow, and big trees are a great age. *OUTDOORS* Wonderful ornamental palms for the tropics and sub-tropics, they appreciate much water during dry spells. *INDOORS* This species is not known to have been tried indoors.

COPERNICIA MACROGLOSSA
CUBAN PETTICOAT PALM

An unmistakable palm, it has stiff erect leaves which, when dead, form a dense skirt.
ORIGIN Cuba.
MATURE HEIGHT To 4.5m/15ft.
TRUNK Solitary, bearing the huge petticoat of dead leaves.
LEAF The large, fan-shaped leaf is deeply cut and stiff.
FLOWER STALK From among the leaf bases.
FRUIT Oval, 18mm/¾in long.
SEED Small, round and wrinkled.
CULTIVATION Although easily germinated from seed, growth is very slow. *OUTDOORS* This is a palm for the tropics or sub-tropics, in sunny well-drained position. *INDOORS* It is not thought to have been tried as a house plant.

CORYPHA ELATA

This is a massive tropical palm. The genus produces the largest flowering structure in the plant kingdom, the huge inflorescence containing millions of flowers.
ORIGIN India, Burma.
MATURE HEIGHT To 21 or 24m/70 or 80ft.
TRUNK Solitary, about 45cm/18in in diameter, sometimes with a faint spiral pattern left by old leaf scars.
LEAF Huge, fan-shaped costapalmate leaf, perhaps 3m (10ft) across, the massive petiole being edged with teeth.
FLOWER STALK The largest inflorescence of any flowering plant, it grows at the very top of the mature tree, and produces millions of flowers; after fruiting, the tree dies.
FRUIT Round, 2.5cm/1in in diameter.
SEED Round, produced in huge numbers.
CULTIVATION This palm is only suitable for large tropical parks and gardens. The big seeds germinate readily, if fresh. *OUTDOORS* These huge trees take up a lot of room, but if space is not a problem, they are a wonderful addition to the tropical garden. *INDOORS* Their requirements indoors are little known, but doubtless seedlings could be grown for a while, given sufficient humidity, warmth and light.

CORYPHA UMBRACULIFERA
TALIPOT PALM

One of the most massive palms, it is a fantastic sight when in flower, with its huge trunk, leaves and inflorescence.
ORIGIN Sri Lanka.
MATURE HEIGHT To 24m/80ft or more.
TRUNK Solitary, 60cm/24in in diameter, usually covered in old leaf bases, and these in turn with epiphytic plants; scars are noticeable where old leaves have fallen.
LEAF Huge costapalmate fan leaf, perhaps 4.5m/15ft across; the petiole armed with teeth along its edge.
FLOWER STALK See notes under *C. elata*.
FRUIT Round, the size of a golf ball, falling in great numbers when ripe.
SEED Large, round.
CULTIVATION See notes under *C. elata*.

CYRTOSTACHYS RENDA
SEALING WAX PALM, RAJAH PALM

A most beautiful and colourful palm, it is quite common in the tropics. *C. lakka* is now synonymous with this species.
ORIGIN Malaysia.
MATURE HEIGHT To 4.5m/15ft.
TRUNK Multiple, slim, distinctly ringed, with brilliant scarlet crownshaft and petioles.
LEAF Feather shaped and quite stiffly held; the red coloration extends along the leafstalk in an unmistakable way.
FLOWER STALK From below the crownshaft.
FRUIT Small, 18mm/¾in, black when ripe.
SEED 12mm/½in, oval.
CULTIVATION The small seeds germinate quickly if fresh, but otherwise they can take several months. Definitely tropical in its requirements, it is slow growing, but worth the wait. *OUTDOORS* A wonderful palm for the tropical garden, it can take either full sun or shade, and requires adequate water. *INDOORS* Although a tempting subject, it is almost impossible to grow as a house plant, because of its tropical requirements.

DAEMONOROPS ANGUSTIFOLIA

This climbing rattan palm is equipped with sharp hooks and spines, which enable it to struggle up through other foliage in the rainforest.
ORIGIN Malaysia.
MATURE HEIGHT Determined by the surrounding vegetation, but may be very great indeed.
TRUNK Very slim, and covered in sharp spines, the stems of *Daemonorops* are used, after cleaning and sorting, to make rattan furniture and other items.
LEAF Rather pretty and regular, feather-shaped leaf, with the central stem extending way beyond the leaf tip, and modified into a climbing aid (a "cirrus") with many backward-facing hooks, which should be treated with respect as they are quite dangerous.
FLOWER STALK Grows from between the leaf bases.
FRUIT Rather attractive, covered with overlapping scales, sometimes oozing a red liquid called "dragon's blood".
SEED Small, round.
CULTIVATION The small seeds germinate readily if fresh. *OUTDOORS* Care should be exercised because of its dangerous nature, but it is perfectly possible to grow this palm in the wet tropics. *INDOORS* Its regular leaflets would make it an attractive house plant, which could be grown for a few years. Humidity is essential.

*D*ECKENIA NOBILIS
PALMISTE

A beautiful, tall palm from the Seychelles, it is rare in its natural habitat, and also in cultivation, though occasional specimens may be found in botanic gardens.
ORIGIN Seychelles Islands.
MATURE HEIGHT To 30m/100ft.
TRUNK Slim, closely ringed, covered – when young – with sharp spines, a feature not seen on older trees.
LEAF Feather shaped, their bases forming a crownshaft.
FLOWER STALK From below the crownshaft.
FRUIT 12mm/½in long, approximately heart shaped; black when ripe.
SEED Roughly heart shaped.
CULTIVATION Seeds germinate quickly and easily if very fresh.
OUTDOORS This is well worth trying for its rarity alone, though tropical conditions are certainly required. *INDOORS* Nothing is known of its requirements as a house plant.

*D*ICTYOSPERMA ALBUM
PRINCESS PALM; HURRICANE PALM

This is reasonably common in cultivation, small plants sometimes even being available in supermarkets, but it is very rare in the wild. A red form – *D. album* var. *rubrum* – is also seen.
ORIGIN Mascarene Islands.
MATURE HEIGHT To around 9m/30ft.
TRUNK Distinctively swollen at the base, grey, solitary, often with vertical fissures; crownshaft.
LEAF Broad and feather shaped.
FLOWER STALK From below the crownshaft.
FRUIT 18mm/¾in long, egg shaped, dark red to black when ripe.
SEED Egg shaped, pointed, with scar from one end to the other.
CULTIVATION The seeds germinate quickly and easily. *OUTDOORS* This palm makes a handsome addition to any tropical collection. *INDOORS* An attractive house plant, especially the red variety, it likes warmth and humidity, but not cold.

ELAEIS GUINEENSIS

Why is the oil palm so called? The answer is that one of the most important vegetable oils in the world is produced by this rather untidy palm. Originally from Africa, it is now widespread throughout the tropics and is grown by the million for this important crop. Sometimes you can drive for hours without seeing anything other than plantations of this tree.

The fruit, from which the oil comes, is produced when the tree is comparatively young, and genetic engineering has played its part in this acceleration of nature. The fruits are produced in large and heavy clusters, which are cut out of the crown of the tree with a special long-handled knife. Rats and snakes also live alongside the fruits, so this is not the most pleasant of jobs. The fruit clumps are then barrowed to the roadside to await collection by trucks.

At the factory, immensely strong crushing machines are used to extract the oil, which is then moved by tanker lorries. It is a huge industry, worth millions of dollars annually, and is one of the biggest exports of many tropical countries.

ELAEIS GUINEENSIS
OIL PALM

Planted commercially by the million in tropical countries for the edible oil contained in the fruit and seeds, it is rapidly replacing the rainforests in Malaysia.
ORIGIN West Africa.
MATURE HEIGHT To 18 or 21m/60 or 70ft, usually much less in cultivated specimens.
TRUNK To 45cm/18in thick, covered with untidy old leaf bases and often epiphytic plants and ferns.
LEAF Feather shaped, the leaflets being in two planes, giving a slightly plumose appearance.
FLOWER STALK From among the leaf bases.
FRUIT In large, tight bunches, yellow, then red, and finally glossy black at maturity; an extremely important tropical crop in many countries, plantations covering hundreds of square miles.
SEED 2.5cm/1in, very hard, pointed at one end.
CULTIVATION The hard seeds germinate with some difficulty. *OUTDOORS* Not a very attractive palm, it must be said, it is, however, easily grown in the tropics. *INDOORS* The oil palm can be grown on for a few years as a young plant, requiring warmth and humidity for good results.

EUGEISSONA TRISTIS
BERTAM

Locally a very common palm, it is unusual outside its native habitat, and is not often seen even in botanic gardens. It is a forest pest in some areas, where it forms great colonies to the exclusion of all other plants.
ORIGIN Malaysia.
MATURE HEIGHT To 7.5m/25ft.
TRUNK None, the leaves rising directly from the underground stem; these palms form large, untidy clumps.
LEAF To 7.5m/25ft long, feather shaped, stalks spiny.
FLOWER STALK Curious woody flower stalk rising erect from among the leaves.
FRUIT Large, 5cm/2in long by 2.5cm/1in, oval, pointed at both ends, covered with tiny scales.
SEED Oval, with deep ridges and grooves along its length.
CULTIVATION The large seeds germinate in eight to ten weeks. *OUTDOORS* A tropical climate with seasonally dry conditions is best for this palm. *INDOORS* Nothing is known of its indoor requirements.

EUTERPE EDULIS
ASSAI PALM

An important crop-palm in South America, where it is grown for "heart of palm" or "palmito", it sometimes appears on the house plant market, as an attractive small palm.
ORIGIN Brazil.
MATURE HEIGHT To 24m/80ft.
TRUNK Slim and attractive, with a prominent green crownshaft.
LEAF Elegant, feather leaf, with many narrow leaflets.
FLOWER STALK From below crownshaft.
FRUIT Round, 12mm/½in, almost black when ripe.
SEED Round.
CULTIVATION Fresh seeds germinate readily. *OUTDOORS* The assai palm prefers tropical conditions, although there is some evidence that this species can grow well in cooler climates. *INDOORS* An excellent house plant, it is tolerant of low light and is easily cared for. It is usual, and best, to plant several to a pot.

GASTROCOCOS CRISPA
CUBAN BELLY PALM

This striking and unusual palm has a swollen trunk, which gives it its common name.
ORIGIN Cuba.
MATURE HEIGHT To 13.5m/45ft.
TRUNK Solitary, smooth and ringed, swollen about or above the middle, and very spiny.
LEAF Feather, dark green above, paler beneath, with a spiny petiole.
FLOWER STALK From among the leaves.
FRUIT 2.5cm/1in in diameter.
SEED Small, round.
CULTIVATION The small seeds are erratic to germinate, but subsequent growth is reasonably fast. *OUTDOORS* Tropical to subtropical climates, and full sun, would suit this handsome palm best. *INDOORS* It is not known to have been tried as a house plant.

GUIHAYAIA ARGYRATA

Pronounced "Gwee-higher", this is a recently described, attractive palm from southern China, where it grows in tiny crevices, often on sheer rock faces. Perhaps it is totally non-competitive and these are thus the only sites available to it. It is hoped that this attractive palm will become more common as its potential is explored.
ORIGIN South China, quite common in the Guilin area.
MATURE HEIGHT A few feet.
TRUNK The plant is usually stunted by the situation of its growth, and thus trunkless; in better conditions a small trunk may emerge.
LEAF Unique among palms, it is fan shaped, with reduplicate (roof- as opposed to valley-shaped) leaflets; it also has a brilliant white-silvery back to the leaf, unsuspected when seen from above.
FLOWER STALK From among the leaf bases.
FRUIT Small, round, black when ripe.
SEED Small, round.
CULTIVATION The small seeds germinate erratically. *OUTDOORS* It would presumably require dry conditions, and certainly full sun. Very slow growing in its natural habitat, it is probably faster in cultivation, and could be grown in a tropical, subtropical, or warm temperate climate. *INDOORS* Well worth trying if and when available, bright light, and drying-out between waterings are probably essential.

HEDESCEPE CANTERBURYANA
UMBRELLA PALM

This grows on exposed and windswept ridges of its island home, and is thus ideal for planting in coastal areas.
ORIGIN Lord Howe Island, a tiny dot in the ocean off the east coast of Australia; this is also the home of the howeas.
MATURE HEIGHT To 7.5m/25ft.
TRUNK Solitary, grey, with crownshaft.
LEAF Not unlike the kentia palm leaf, being feather-shaped, coarse, and dark green.
FLOWER STALK From below the crownshaft.
FRUIT Large, up to 5cm/2in long, oval, and dark red when ripe.
SEED Large, slightly longer than wide, with a characteristic broad scar down one side.
CULTIVATION Seeds are difficult and erratic to germinate. *OUTDOORS* Good for exposed position, it is slow growing, but will tolerate high winds and salt spray. *INDOORS* An excellent indoor palm, it is tolerant of low light and slow growing.

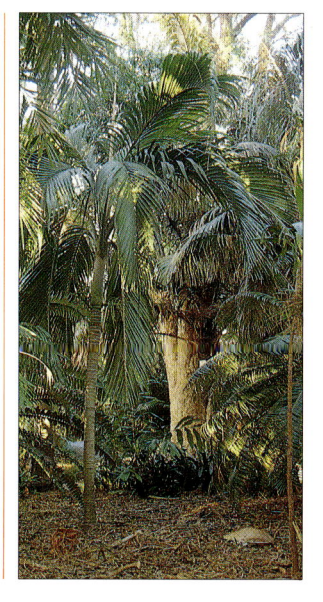

HOWEA BELMOREANA
SENTRY PALM

This is well known, mainly because of its more famous brother, the kentia palm, *H. forsteriana*, to which it is similar in many respects.
ORIGIN Lord Howe Island, off eastern Australia.
MATURE HEIGHT To 7.5m/25ft.
TRUNK Slim, dark green in young plants, grey in older trees, ringed with old leaf scars; no crownshaft.
LEAF Dark green, leathery texture, feather shaped, with the leaflets pointing upwards forming a "V" shape.
FLOWER STALK A single spike, pendulous, from below lowest leaves; the stalks of several seasons may be on the tree at the same time, the pollen from one fertilizing the flowers on the previous season's flower stalk below.
FRUIT The size and shape of an olive, but sharper at each end; takes two years to ripen, at which time it turns from green to dark brown.
SEED Oval.
CULTIVATION The seeds are slow and erratic to germinate, and it is essential that they are fresh. *OUTDOORS* It is a palm for temperate and warm temperate areas and will not do well in the tropics, seeming to enjoy fresh air and breezy conditions. It must have shade when young, but will later tolerate full sun. *INDOORS* Not as popular as its relative, it is still very useful indoors, where it tolerates low light and neglect.

HOWEA FORSTERIANA
KENTIA PALM

One of the most popular and indeed most suitable palms in the world for interior use, it was introduced into Europe during Victorian times, and has been popular ever since. It was used by the Victorians to good effect for their "Palm Court orchestras".

ORIGIN Lord Howe Island, off the east coast of Australia.
MATURE HEIGHT To 15m/50ft.
TRUNK Slim, dark green with prominent rings when young, grey and less prominently ringed when older.
LEAF Broad, dark green, feather shaped, leathery texture, leaflets held in a flat plane and not rising upwards, like those of *H. belmoreana*.
FLOWER STALK From below the lowest leaves, multiple; several seasons' stalks may be on the trunk at any one time, pollen from one falling to fertilize the last season's flowers below.
FRUIT Bigger than *H. belmoreana*, but similar in shape; dark brown when ripe, which can take two years.
SEED Oval, a little larger than those of *H. belmoreana*.
CULTIVATION Seeds are again erratic and difficult to germinate, and should be absolutely fresh for best results. *OUTDOORS* It requires a sunny position in temperate or warm temperate areas, and shade when young. *INDOORS* Unsurpassed as an indoor subject, it will tolerate low light and general abuse.

HYDRIASTELE MICROSPADIX

A pretty, slim, clump-forming, tropical palm, with distinctive arrangements of leaflets, it is worthy of greater use.

ORIGIN New Guinea.
MATURE HEIGHT To 12m/40ft.
TRUNK Several, slim, forming an attractive clump; crownshaft.
LEAF Feather shaped, with an irregular arrangement of both narrow and broad leaflets with squared-off ends, most noticeable in silhouette.
FLOWER STALK From below the crownshafts.
FRUIT Small, round, bright red when ripe.
SEED Small, 12mm/½in round, covered with fibres.
CULTIVATION The small seeds germinate easily, but may take some months to do so and must be fresh. *OUTDOORS* A useful, small clumping palm for the moist tropics. *INDOORS* It is not known to be used in the home.

PALM IDENTIFIER

HYOPHORBE LAGENICAULIS
BOTTLE PALM

This unusual palm is well named, as its trunk really is the shape of a bottle. It is virtually extinct in the wild.
ORIGIN Mascarene Islands.
MATURE HEIGHT To only about 3m/10ft.
TRUNK The great bulging trunk, sometimes regular with visible rings, sometimes irregular with less noticeable rings, is one of the curiosities of the plant kingdom. This tapers to the point where it forms a crownshaft, itself usually swollen for the first few inches.
LEAF Very stiff, feather shaped, often twisted and recurved; there are only four or five leaves, even on a mature tree.
FLOWER STALK From below the crownshaft.
FRUIT Oval, 4cm/1½in by 2.5cm/1in.
SEED Oval in shape, with raised "veins" on the surface.
CULTIVATION The seeds germinate easily if fresh, though the process may take some weeks, or months. *OUTDOORS* A wonderful subject for the tropical garden, it will tolerate full sun and salt spray, and requires plenty of water. *INDOORS* It is not much used in interiors, although it is very suitable if conditions are warm enough, and there is sufficient light.

HYOPHORBE VERSCHAFFELTII
SPINDLE PALM

A close relative of *H. lagenicaulis,* it is distinguished by the different shape of its trunk. A very attractive palm, and planted widely in the tropics, it is occasionally used in interiors, where it commands much attention.
ORIGIN Mascarene Islands, where it is almost extinct in the wild state.
MATURE HEIGHT To 6m/20ft.
TRUNK Spindle shaped (narrow at the base), becoming wider half way up, and then tapering again to the swollen crown shaft; rings or scars left by old leaves.
LEAF Quite stiff, more erect and less recurved than the bottle palm, otherwise similar.
FLOWER STALK From below the swollen crownshaft.
FRUIT 2.5cm/1in, oval.
SEED Long and narrow.
CULTIVATION The seeds may take several weeks or months to germinate, and care should be taken that they are fresh. *OUTDOORS* A showy and unusual palm for tropical locations, it needs full sun and sufficient moisture. *INDOORS* This is a good palm for indoor use, but requires warmth and good light.

45

Hyphaene dichotoma
DOUM PALM

One of the few truly branching palms, and regarded as a curiosity because of it. In its own way, this unmistakable palm is a beautiful tree, but only rarely seen. A palm of the dry and arid plains and semi-deserts.
ORIGIN East coast of India.
MATURE HEIGHT To 18m/60ft.
TRUNK Slender but much branched, each branch dividing again and again, and ending in a crown of leaves.
LEAF Heavily costapalmate, that is, the petiole extending into the leaf blade and giving a twisted appearance; the leaf itself is hard, waxy and durable.
FLOWER STALK From among the leaf bases.
FRUIT The shape and size of a pear, very hard, and an orange-brown colour.
SEED Extremely difficult to extract from the fruit, being very hard and bony.
CULTIVATION The large seeds can germinate extremely quickly, or can sometimes take many weeks. They require a deep pot, as the first root grows very long as it seeks out ground moisture. *OUTDOORS* An unusual, slow-growing ornamental for hot and dry areas, it will also grow in the humid tropics. *INDOORS* Nothing is known of its indoor requirements, but its need for bright light would be a limiting factor.

Johannestejsmannia altifrons

A wonderful and fabulous tropical palm, its huge undivided leaves are much prized as thatching in its native land.
ORIGIN Malaysia.
MATURE HEIGHT To about 3m/10ft.
TRUNK None, the leaves rising direct from an underground stem.
LEAF Huge, simple, to 1.8–2.1m/6 or 7ft long and 60 or 90cm/ 2 or 3ft wide.
FLOWER STALK From among the leaf bases.
FRUIT Round, about 2.5cm/1in, with a warty, corky surface.
SEED Round and slightly flattened.
CULTIVATION This exciting palm is becoming more common in botanical collections, and deserves to be more widely grown. The seeds must be fresh and are erratic to germinate. *OUTDOORS* Requiring a shaded position in the moist tropics, it is slow growing, but well worth the wait. It is essential to afford protection from wind, which would easily damage the huge leaves. *INDOORS* Plants would probably only survive in a hot and moist greenhouse, which closely imitates the tropical conditions they require.

JUBAEA CHILENSIS

This huge palm tree (it has the thickest trunk of any palm), once common in its native Chile, has been over-exploited in the past for the manufacture of "palm wine". A mature trunk can contain up to 100 gallons of sugary sap, which is boiled down to make palm honey, or fermented to produce the alcoholic liquor. The collection of this sap results in the death of the tree, and it is now rare in some areas where it was once the main component of the vegetation.

Fortunately, it is now a protected tree in its native country, and it is also being extensively replanted for the production of the nuts, called "coquitos" (little coconuts), which are both edible and delicious, tasting just like real coconuts (*Cocos nucifera*).

JUBAEA CHILENSIS
CHILEAN WINE PALM

A palm of awesome size – unmistakable with its massive trunk – it is much planted in botanic gardens and public parks in most of the warm temperate parts of the world. In its native Chile, a wine is made from the sap.

ORIGIN Chile, where it is now endangered, due to excessive felling.
MATURE HEIGHT To 21m/70ft.
TRUNK Massive, to 1.5 or 1.8m/5 or 6ft in diameter, grey, smooth, with faint flattened diamond-shaped old leaf scars; no crownshaft.
LEAF Feather, coarse, leathery texture, leaflets reduplicate (roof as opposed to valley shaped).
FLOWER STALK From among the leaves.
FRUIT Round, 4cm/1½in in diameter, yellow.
SEED 2.5cm/1in in circumference, hard and bony, with an edible flesh, tasting like coconut.
CULTIVATION If fresh, the large seeds germinate without additional heat in a few months. *OUTDOORS* Not happy in the tropics, this is an essential palm for all warm temperate regions, and will tolerate severe cold and frost once established. As it is very slow growing, it is usually future generations that benefit from the planting of this wonderful palm. *INDOORS* It can be grown indoors, but needs bright, indirect light, and is extremely slow growing.

JUBAEAOPSIS CAFFRA
PONDOLAND PALM

This rarely-encountered palm is now creating more attention, and is occasionally seen in collections. It is related to the *Jubaea* genus.
ORIGIN North-eastern South Africa, restricted to only a few sites, where it grows on river banks.
MATURE HEIGHT To 6m/20ft.
TRUNK Multiple, slim, covered with old leaf scars.
LEAF Feather, coarse textured and leathery.
FLOWER STALKS From among the leaves.
FRUIT Like *Jubaea* in many respects.
SEED Very similar to *Jubaea*.
CULTIVATION This has not been much tried, firstly because seeds are difficult to obtain (many trees overhang the water and the seeds are lost), and secondly because they are extremely difficult to germinate. *OUTDOORS* The Pondoland palm would require a warm and sunny position, with adequate water. *INDOORS* It is not known to have been tried indoors.

LACCOSPADIX AUSTRALASICA
ATHERTON PALM

An Australian palm, rapidly gaining popularity in that country as a house plant, it will undoubtedly become more available in future years, but at present is rare outside of its native home.
ORIGIN North-East Australia, in rainforests.
MATURE HEIGHT To 3m/10ft.
TRUNK Slim, solitary or multiple, dark green, ringed.
LEAF Feather, delicate in appearance.
FLOWER STALK From among the leaf bases.
FRUIT Very pretty, hanging on pendulous single spikes, bright red when ripe.
SEED Small, round.
CULTIVATION This is excellent either for indoors or outdoors (in temperate to tropical zones). The small seeds may be erratic in germination and the young plants grow slowly. It is not thought to be frost hardy. *OUTDOORS* A moist, shady area in the garden, with a steady supply of water at all times, would suit this attractive small palm. *INDOORS* A wonderful indoor palm, it will tolerate much-reduced light levels and should be treated in the same way as a chameadorea.

LATANIA LODDIGESSII
BLUE LATAN PALM

Three beautiful and distinct stiff-leaved fan palms form the *Latania* genus. Though common in cultivation, they are thought to be almost extinct in their native home.
ORIGIN Mascarene Islands.
MATURE HEIGHT To 12m/40ft.
TRUNK Slim, grey, ringed indistinctly with scars of old leaves.
LEAF Very stiff, fan-shaped leaves, glaucous blue green in colour, costapalmate (the leaf stalk extends well into the leaf); the bases divide into two where they join the trunk.
FLOWER STALK From among the leaf bases.
FRUIT Large and plum-like, dark brown when ripe, usually containing three seeds per fruit.
SEED Interestingly sculpted, broader at one end, and looking as though carved; a prominent ridge runs along the length.
CULTIVATION Plants are easily grown from seed, which germinates in a few weeks if fresh. *OUTDOORS* A sunny position in tropics or sub-tropics is required, together with adequate water in dry weather, and a well-drained soil. Plants can be quite fast growing. *INDOORS* This shows some promise as an interior plant, but it requires good bright light, and benefits from humidity, though the latter appears not to be essential.

LATANIA LONTAROIDES
RED LATAN PALM

The young plants have a beautiful red coloration on the leaves and leaf stalks. An attractive and strong-growing palm, it is not uncommon in cultivation.
ORIGIN Reunion Island, where it is almost extinct.
MATURE HEIGHT To 12m/40ft.
TRUNK Slim, solitary, grey, about 20cm/8in in diameter.
LEAF Stiff fan-shaped, costapalmate leaves, with red-purple coloration, especially in juvenile plants.
FLOWER STALK From among the leaf bases.
FRUIT Large and plum-like, dark brown when ripe.
SEED Round at one end, pointed at the other; "sculpturing" much less apparent than with the other two species.
CULTIVATION The seeds germinate easily if fresh, but may take several weeks. *OUTDOORS* This is another wonderful palm for the tropical or subtropical garden; sun, good drainage and adequate watering in dry weather will promote good growth. *INDOORS* While it is not known to be used as a house plant, it would be well worth a try. Bright light would certainly be required.

LATANIA VERSCHAFFELTII
YELLOW LATAN PALM

Its quite striking yellow coloration easily identifies this attractive, tropical palm.
ORIGIN Rodrigues Island in the Indian Ocean, where it is now extremely rare.
MATURE HEIGHT To 12m/40ft.
TRUNK Slim, grey, solitary, old leaf scars leaving rings.
LEAF Hard and durable, strong yellow or golden coloration of the leaf stalk, and veins, especially noticeable in younger plants; costapalmate.
FLOWER STALK From among the leaf bases.
FRUIT Large, the shape and size of a plum, brown when ripe.
SEED Looking as though sculptured, or moulded, with ridges in a quite intricate pattern, beaked at one end.
CULTIVATION Easily cultivated from seed, which germinates in a few weeks or months. *OUTDOORS* A sunny position in the tropical or sub-tropical garden would suit this palm best, and although they show some resistance to drought, adequate watering during dry weather would be beneficial. *INDOORS* Not thought to be grown indoors, it would perhaps do well, given enough light and warmth.

LICUALA GRANDIS
RUFFLED FAN PALM

Immediately recognizable for its beautiful leaves, *Licuala grandis* is but one in a genus of over 100 species. Essentially a tropical palm, it is occasionally seen for sale as a house plant.
ORIGIN New Hebrides, a group of islands off the north coast of Australia.
MATURE HEIGHT To 2.4 or 2.7m/8 or 9ft.
TRUNK Slim, solitary, a few inches only in diameter, grey.
LEAF Unmistakable: a beautiful, circular, undivided and regularly pleated leaf, about 60cm/24in in diameter or more, with a notched edge.
FLOWER STALK From among the leaf bases.
FRUIT Bright red when ripe, small and round.
SEED Small, round, with a segmented appearance, like a peeled orange.
CULTIVATION Essentially a tropical palm, its small seeds germinate in a few weeks – without difficulty, if fresh. *OUTDOORS* A sunny or shaded position in the humid, tropical garden is the ideal spot for this small palm tree. *INDOORS* It may certainly be grown indoors, but steps must be taken to ensure adequate humidity, and warmth. Air that is too dry invariably results in the edges of the leaves browning. The best places in the home are probably the bathroom or kitchen.

LICUALA ORBICULARIS

Perhaps the most beautiful of the licualas, and thus of the palms, its leaf has to be seen to be believed. One unfortunate local use is as a temporary umbrella – it is heartbreaking to see leaves discarded after a brief shower.
ORIGIN Borneo.
MATURE HEIGHT To 3m/10ft perhaps.
TRUNK None, the leaf stalks rising direct from the underground rootstock.
LEAF Circular and glossy, to 90cm or 1.2m/3 or 4ft in diameter, and held flat, unlike *L. grandis,* which is undulating – fabulous!
FLOWER STALK From among the leaf bases.
FRUIT Round, 12mm/½in in diameter, red when ripe.
SEED Small, round.
CULTIVATION The seeds, which are slowly becoming more available, germinate in a few weeks or months. Subsequent seedling growth is slow. *OUTDOORS* Shelter from wind is the most important condition for this beautiful palm. The slightest breeze will ruin the huge leaves. It is absolutely tropical in its other requirements. *INDOORS* It's tempting to try this palm as an interior subject, but do so only if you can provide year-round warmth and high humidity, for instance in a tropical glasshouse. Low to medium light is preferred.

LICUALA SPINOSA

Its relationship to *L. grandis* is easily seen; its leaf looks much like a split-up ruffled fan leaf, and it is perhaps the best licuala for interior use.
ORIGIN From southern Thailand, down through Malaysia, to western Indonesia.
MATURE HEIGHT To 3.6 or 3.9m/12 or 13ft.
TRUNK Multiple, slim, clustering, ending up as a dense bush.
LEAF Circular in shape, but divided to the base into irregular leaflets, with squared-off ends; the very first seedling leaf also has a squared tip.
FLOWER STALK From among the leaf bases.
FRUIT Round, the size of a marble, red when ripe.
SEED Small and round.
CULTIVATION If fresh, the seeds will germinate within a few weeks or months. *OUTDOORS* Though again a tropical species, *L. spinosa* wil also succeed in the sub-tropics. *INDOORS* This is perhaps the most successful of the licualas for use indoors, where it seems slightly less fussy about humidity. Also, the leaves are thicker and more leathery and thus resist dry air better. Medium to low light is tolerated well.

LIVISTONA AUSTRALIS
AUSTRALIAN FAN PALM

This is one of a genus containing some 30 species, distributed from the Middle East through South-East Asia to Australia. Many are cultivated as ornamental plants, from temperate to tropical zones.

ORIGIN Eastern Australia – it is thus one of the most southerly-growing palms in the world.
MATURE HEIGHT To 15m/50ft.
TRUNK Solitary, grey, about 30cm/12in in diameter.
LEAF Fan shaped, with distinctively drooping tips; the petiole (leaf stalk) is edged with very sharp teeth.
FLOWER STALK From among the leaves.
FRUIT Round, 18mm/¾in in diameter, red brown when ripe.
SEED Round, 12mm/½in in diameter.
CULTIVATION The seeds germinate quickly and easily, and subsequent seedling growth is quite fast. *OUTDOORS* Growing in climates from temperate to tropical, it prefers full sun but can do well in shade and well-drained soil, with an adequate supply of water in dry weather. *INDOORS* It is perfectly possible to grow this palm indoors, but it requires bright, indirect light.

LIVISTONA CHINENSIS
CHINESE FAN PALM, FOUNTAIN PALM

This is a popular species, both as an indoor and an outdoor specimen.
ORIGIN Southern China.
MATURE HEIGHT To 12m/40ft.
TRUNK Solitary, some 30cm/12in in diameter, often enlarged at the base; grey in colour, with barely distinguishable rings.
LEAF Fan shaped, longer than wide, with a spiny petiole, and strongly drooping leaf tips, earning it the common name of fountain palm.
FLOWER STALK From among the leaf bases.
FRUIT Oval, dark green in colour, 2.5cm/1in in length.
SEED Oval, pale brown in colour, 18mm/¾in long.
CULTIVATION The fountain palm is easily cultivated from seed, which germinates readily and quickly. *OUTDOORS* It is a popular palm in all areas, from temperate to tropical; full sun, and adequate water in dry weather will ensure success. *INDOORS* Equally popular as a house plant, it requires bright, indirect light.

LIVISTONA ROTUNDIFOLIA
FOOTSTOOL PALM

A distinctive livistona, somewhat more tropical in its requirements than the others, it is generally more tidy in appearance.
ORIGIN Malaysia, Indonesia, Philippines.
MATURE HEIGHT To 15m/50ft.
TRUNK Slim, pale grey, some forms having a distinctively ringed trunk, though this is uncommon; only some 20cm/8in in diameter.
LEAF Fan shaped, round and very regular in appearance, often forming a deep crown, much taller than wide.
FLOWER STALK From among the leaf bases.
FRUIT 18mm/^{3}/$_4$in round, and red brown when ripe.
SEED 12mm/^{1}/$_2$in in circumference, pale brown.
CULTIVATION The seeds germinate easily and quickly. *OUTDOORS* This is a beautiful fan palm for the tropics, especially the more unusual forms, which are worth seeking out. *INDOORS* The young plants are very attractive, with their regular, shallowly-divided leaves, their main requirements being bright, indirect light, and an adequate supply of water.

LODOICEA MALDIVICA
COCO-DE-MER, DOUBLE COCONUT

This fabulous palm bears the largest seed in the vegetable kingdom, a single one weighing up to 18kg/40lb.
ORIGIN Unique to the Seychelles Islands in the Indian Ocean.
MATURE HEIGHT To 24m/80ft.
TRUNK Solitary, very tall, but not especially thick.
LEAF Very large, fan shaped, strongly costapalmate; in the valleys where they grow, the huge leaves crash into one another during gales, making an awesome noise.
FLOWER STALK From among the leaf bases.
FRUIT Very large, up to 37.5cm/15in long, taking five years to ripen.
SEED Looking like a 2-lobed coconut, the largest seed in the world, and the heaviest.
CULTIVATION Seeds are difficult to obtain, and expensive. They need to be planted in their permanent position as they produce a long taproot. Alternatively, they can be started off in a large pot. They may take over a year to germinate. *OUTDOORS* This is a palm for the humid tropics, but even in this region they are considered difficult to establish. *INDOORS* Attempts have been made to grow them in tropical glasshouses, with some success. Even the very first leaf is huge, and much space is therefore required.

LYTOCARYUM WEDDELLIANUM
MINIATURE COCONUT PALM

Formerly listed as *Microcoeleum Weddellianum*, this is a graceful and dainty palm, most often seen as a small pot plant, and as such they are sold by the thousand in garden centres and supermarkets.
ORIGIN Brazil.
MATURE HEIGHT Only to about 1.8m/6ft.
TRUNK Only about 5cm/2in thick, often much less, and ringed.
LEAF Very fine and delicate feather leaf, with fine leaflets a glossy green in colour.
FLOWER STALK From among the leaf bases.
FRUIT 18mm/¾in in circumference, looking like a tiny coconut.
SEED 12mm/½in in diameter, with three pores, or "eyes".
CULTIVATION The small seeds germinate within a few weeks. *OUTDOORS* A shady position in the subtropical garden would be ideal. Humidity is appreciated and keeps the plant looking fresh. Although slow growing, it is well worth the wait, as it is surely one of the most beautiful of the small palms. It will also grow in cooler, but frost-free, areas. Shade is essential, and the extremely fragile roots make it almost impossible to transplant. *INDOORS* A popular house plant, it is usually grown commercially in clay pots without drainage holes to avoid the necessity of cutting the roots, which would mean the death of the plant. It is tolerant of low light, and appreciative of humidity.

METROXYLON SAGU
SAGO PALM

Easily recognizable for its erect habit, and its fruits, it is an important source of sago in its native home, and often seen around villages in the tropics. The trunks are felled as they are about to flower, and the sago is extracted from the split trunk.
ORIGIN South-East Asia.
MATURE HEIGHT To 9m/30ft.
TRUNK Clump forming, with one or two main stems; each trunk dies after fruiting, to be replaced by others.
LEAF Feather shaped, held stiffly upright, curving gently out towards the top, which gives the species a distinctive silhouette.
FLOWER STALK Produced terminally from the top of the trunk, in the manner of the *Corypha* genus.
FRUIT The size of a golf ball, pear shaped, covered with attractive overlapping scales, like the skin of a reptile.
SEED 4cm/1½in in circumference, with one side concave.
CULTIVATION The seeds are difficult and erratic to germinate, and may take some months to do so. *OUTDOORS* This is very much a palm for the tropics, where it is happy in moist (even swampy) ground in full sun. The fact that it is fast growing, and that it dies after fruiting, may be a disadvantage for the gardener. *INDOORS* Nothing is known of its indoor requirements.

PALM IDENTIFIER

NANNORRHOPS RITCHIANA
MAZARI PALM

This is a mystery palm, in so far as it is extremely common in its native homelands, but extremely rare in cultivation, and is only now slowly finding its way on to specialists' lists. There are only a handful of mature plants in both America and Europe.
ORIGIN Arid areas of Afghanistan, Pakistan, Saudi Arabia, Iran.
MATURE HEIGHT To 6m/20ft.
TRUNK Multiple, sometimes prostrate, as if too heavy to support itself, sometimes erect, sometimes branched; about 30cm/12in in diameter.
LEAF Stiff, fan-shaped leaf, costapalmate, blue grey in colour.
FLOWER STALK Flowering is terminal, but does not result in the death of the plant, as the next fork down takes over.
FRUIT 18mm/¾in in diameter, red brown when ripe.
SEED Round, 12mm/½in in diameter, very hard, with a small central cavity.
CULTIVATION The seeds, given adequate heat, begin to germinate rapidly, but this process may continue over many months. *OUTDOORS* Hot, dry and bright would summarize this palm's requirements. A well-drained soil, but with an adequate supply of water is also beneficial. It is extremely cold tolerant, a feature largely due to its desert habitat.
INDOORS It would probably make a good conservatory subject, as it thrives in hot, dry air, and bright light.

NEODYPSIS DECARYI
TRIANGLE PALM

An instantly recognizable palm, it is rapidly gaining in popularity, but becoming rare in its native home due to excessive seed exports.
ORIGIN Madagascar.
MATURE HEIGHT To 6m/20ft.
TRUNK The leaf bases form a unique triangular shape at the top of the trunk; below this, the trunks is conventionally round, about 30cm/12in in diameter.
LEAF Long and elegant, a silvery green in colour, feather shaped, and drooping at the tips, forming three distinct ranks even on young plants; the new spear is covered with a dark reddish-brown velvet, as on deer's antlers.
FLOWER STALK From among the leaf bases.
FRUIT 18mm/¾in, oval.
SEED 12mm/½in in diameter, round.
CULTIVATION This is a wonderful palm for both indoor and outdoor use. *OUTDOORS* Extremely drought-tolerant, it should be grown in full sun. Shade-grown specimens tend to be very attenuated and are much less attractive. Be careful not to over-fertilize, as this leads to rapid browning of the leaf tips. *INDOORS* An unsurpassed palm for indoor use, it tolerates low to medium light (though it prefers brighter, indirect light). Its triangular shape means that it can easily be stood against a wall, or in a corner.

55

NORMANBYA NORMANBYI
BLACK PALM

A beautiful Australian native, it has plumose leaves like bottle brushes.
ORIGIN Tropical north-eastern Australia.
MATURE HEIGHT To 15m/50ft.
TRUNK Slim, grey, composed of a very hard black wood, from which it gets its name; crownshaft.
LEAF Attractive and plumose (leaflets at different angles to the leaf stem); wide and coarse leaflets.
FLOWER STALK From below the crownshaft.
FRUIT Egg shaped, 4cm/1½in long, beautiful pink colour when ripe.
SEED Round at one end, pointed at the other.
CULTIVATION Some seeds germinate very quickly if fresh, but often there is a low success rate. *OUTDOORS* The black palm requires tropical to sub-tropical habitat, rich soil, and plenty of water in dry periods. *INDOORS* Although not much tried, it shows promise as a house plant. Humidity must be maintained.

NYPA FRUTICANS
NIPAH PALM

This palm is so different from all the others that for a long time it was not considered to be a palm at all. It is commonly seen in the tropics, where it lines coast and river.
ORIGIN Coastal, swampy, tropical areas from India to Australia.
MATURE HEIGHT To 7.5m/25ft.
TRUNK Subterranean, or indeed submarine, sometimes forking.
LEAF Very long and erect, feather shaped, with a strong, round leaf stalk.
FLOWER STALK A unique vertically-held structure, like a football on a stalk.
FRUIT Much like those of *Pandanus* species, roughly wedge-shaped, so that all the seeds can fit together in a ball shape; 7.5cm/3in long.
SEED Covered in fibre, walnut sized, and edible.
CULTIVATION Culture away from their native home seems to present difficulties; the seeds either refuse to germinate, or die soon afterwards. *OUTDOORS* Tropical, marshy conditions are required, with deep mud, or soft soil. This palm tolerates brackish water. *INDOORS* A plant might succeed in a hot and humid glasshouse, but it would otherwise be extremely difficult to grow this atypical palm indoors.

Oncosperma horridum

Distinctive, tropical, tall, clumping palms, they are extremely spiny in all their parts.
ORIGIN Malaysia, Indonesia.
MATURE HEIGHT To 21mm/70ft.
TRUNK Multiple, slim, dark, covered in sharp spines, the clump being quite impossible to penetrate.
LEAF Feather shaped and elegant, the leaflets are held flat.
FLOWER STALK From among the leaf bases.
FRUIT 12mm/½in in diameter, black when ripe.
SEED Small, round.
CULTIVATION The seeds lose their viability very quickly, and need to be planted within days of collection. *OUTDOORS* An attractive palm for the tropical garden, it forms a large clump in time. Its spiny nature may be a problem. *INDOORS* It is not known to be used indoors, but tropical conditions would undoubtedly be required.

Oncosperma tigillarium
NIBUNG PALM

A tall, elegant, clumping palm for the tropics, it is spiny in all its parts, which may prove a deterrent to its use.
ORIGIN South-East Asia.
MATURE HEIGHT To 24m/80ft.
TRUNK Multiple, with as many as 40 or 50 trunks to a clump; trunks are slim and covered in sharp black spines.
LEAF Elegant feather-shaped leaf, with the leaflets drooping down both sides of the leaf stalk, which is also covered in spines.
FLOWER STALK From among the leaf bases, spiny.
FRUIT 18mm/¾in in circumference, black or dark blue when ripe, with a white bloom.
SEED Small, round.
CULTIVATION The seeds need to be absolutely fresh for successful germination, which takes two or three months. *OUTDOORS* This is a large and impressive palm for the moist tropics, but care should be taken in public areas, because of the sharp spines. *INDOORS* It is unlikely to succeed in anything other than a humid glasshouse.

ORANIOPSIS APPENDICULATA

A little known but interesting palm, it was believed until recently to be related to *Orania;* however, it is now known to be closer to *Ceroxylon.* It will undoubtedly become more widespread in the future.
ORIGIN Queensland, Australia, where it grows in dense rainforests.
MATURE HEIGHT To 9m/30ft, but very slow growing.
TRUNK Rather thick and stout, up to 60cm/24in through, with clear rings, the scars left by old leaves, which drop cleanly.
LEAF Feathershaped, held vertical or horizontal, but not drooping, dark green upper surface and silvery underneath.
FLOWER STALK From among the leaf bases.
FRUIT Round, 4cm/1½in in diameter, yellow when ripe.
SEED Large and round.
CULTIVATION Not much notice was taken of this palm until quite recently, when its relationship to *Ceroxylon* was noted, and thus not much is known of its cultural requirements. The seeds are very slow to germinate, and subsequent growth is also extremely slow. *OUTDOORS* It seems to prefer shade, and a situation that is cool and humid. Given this, it should do well in the sub-tropical or warm temperate garden, but is very slow. *INDOORS* Nothing is known of its indoor requirements.

PARAJUBAEA COCOIDES

An exciting and beautiful palm from South America, it is very fast growing, resembling a coconut, but much more cold tolerant. The main problems seem to be firstly, to obtain the seeds, and then to get them to germinate.
ORIGIN Ecuador, where it is quite common, but only in cultivation; not now known in the wild, but thought to come from the Andean slopes.
MATURE HEIGHT To 12m/40ft.
TRUNK Slim, ringed with old leaf scars.
LEAF Attractive feather leaf, with shiny dark green leaflets, silvery underneath.
FLOWER STALK From among the leaf bases.
FRUIT 4cm/1½in, dark green; brown when ripe.
SEED 3.5cm/1¼in long, with three prominent crests at one end.
CULTIVATION The large seeds germinate erratically and with some difficulty. Success is claimed for various techniques, such as alternating day/night temperatures, cracking the hard seed coat, bathing the seeds in pure oxygen on a bed of moist sphagnum moss, or any combination of the above. Once germinated, growth is very fast. *OUTDOORS* Temperate, frost-free conditions suit this palm best, with a position in full sun. It requires cool nights and sunny days, simulating its mountainous home. *INDOORS* It is said to stop growing after the root has made a few circles around the pot, and is certainly more happy in the ground.

PELAGODOXA HENRYANA

A beautiful but extremely rare palm from the South Pacific, it is not dissimilar to *Phoenicophorium*.
ORIGIN The Marquesas Islands, surely the quintessential South Pacific group; it is rare in the wild, and not common even in tropical botanic gardens.
MATURE HEIGHT To 6m/20ft.
TRUNK Slim, solitary, perhaps 15cm/6in in diameter.
LEAF Large, simple and entire, except when split by the wind.
FLOWER STALK Among the leaf bases.
FRUIT Large – the size of a tennis ball – and distinctively warty and corky.
SEED About 2.5cm/1in in diameter, smooth.
CULTIVATION As can be imagined, not much is known about this rare palm, but certainly humid and tropical conditions would be required. The seeds are slow and erratic to germinate. *OUTDOORS* Likely to succeed only in the tropics, it will hopefully become more available in the years to come. *INDOORS* It is not known to have been tried indoors.

PHOENICOPHORIUM BORSIGIANUM

A beautiful, simple-leaved palm similar in many respects to the foregoing *Pelagodoxa*, it is easily distinguished by its seeds and toothed leaflet tips.
ORIGIN Seychelles Islands, Indian Ocean.
MATURE HEIGHT To 12m/40ft.
TRUNK Slim and solitary, covered with spines when young.
LEAF Simple, entire, but subject to damage by the wind, which causes the leaves to split; lthe tips of the leaves are toothed.
FLOWER STALK From among the leaf bases.
FRUIT About 12mm/½in long, and heart shaped.
SEED Slightly smaller, similarly shaped, covered with a few distinctive veins.
CULTIVATION The small seeds germinate well, if very fresh, but quickly lose all viability. *OUTDOORS* Tropical and humid conditions are required. This is not an easy palm to grow, but worth persevering with. *INDOORS* It is not known to be used as a house plant, though it can be grown in the tropical glasshouse, with high humidity.

PHOENIX CANARIENSIS
CANARY ISLAND DATE PALM

One of the most widespread palms in the world, and very common everywhere in warm temperate areas, ranging from the south of France, to Australia and California.
ORIGIN The Canary Islands, off the west coast of Africa.
MATURE HEIGHT To 18m/60ft, usually seen much less.
TRUNK Solitary and very stout, up to 90cm/3ft in diameter, covered with distinctive old leaf scars which form diamond-shaped patterns.
LEAF Mid-green, feather shaped, with valley-, as opposed to roof-shaped, leaflets, which is distinctive of the entire genus; the lower leaflets are developed into long and extremely stiff and sharp spines, which are quite dangerous when handling the plants.
FLOWER STALK From among the leaf bases.
FRUIT To 5cm/2in long and 12mm/½in wide, orange when ripe; inedible.
SEED Typical date-stone shape, but with rounded ends.
CULTIVATION With heat, the seeds germinate easily and quickly, generally within a few weeks. *OUTDOORS* An essential, though perhaps over-used, palm for warm temperate zones, it grows quickly, but requires a lot of space to develop fully. It is tolerant of cold and drought, but prefers full sun. *INDOORS* An excellent indoor palm, with a spiky, architectural appearance, it thrives in bright, indirect light, and tolerates dry air well.

PHOENIX RECLINATA
SENEGAL DATE PALM, AFRICAN DATE PALM

This is a beautiful, clump-forming date palm, the trunks of which lean outward, hence the name.
ORIGIN Equatorial Africa.
MATURE HEIGHT To 9m/30ft.
TRUNK Multiple, slim, covered with old leaf scars; *reclinata* refers to the outward-leaning habit of the trunks.
LEAF Not dissimilar to that of *P. canariensis*, but only about half as long.
FLOWER STALK From among the leaf bases.
FRUIT Oval in shape, about 18mm/¾in long; brown when ripe.
SEED 12mm/½in long, grooved, round ended.
CULTIVATION This tropical palm will also succeed in warm temperate areas, but does not like frost and cold. The seeds sprout easily and quickly. *OUTDOORS* A beautiful clumping palm, it is tough and tolerant. *INDOORS* Although undoubtedly suitable, when a young plant, for indoor use, it has not been much tried.

PHOENIX DACTYLIFERA

This useful palm is widespread throughout the Middle East and the drier tropics, and its fruit, the well-known date, has been harvested for centuries. Dates can be dried, and kept without deterioration for long periods of time. The male and female flowers are on separate trees, but the males produce pollen in such huge quantities that only one male tree is required for every 100 females. During the season when pollen is produced, the slightest breeze can waft clouds and clouds of pollen, like a yellow mist, drifting across the sand. A good female tree can produce up to 45kg/100lb of fruit per year, and palm wine "toddy" can be produced from the sap collected from unopened flower stalks. Commercially, date palms are produced from the suckers which readily sprout from the base of the tree.

PHOENIX DACTYLIFERA
DATE PALM

This is the date palm of commerce, grown by the million in Middle Eastern countries, and elsewhere, for its delicious and abundant fruit.
ORIGIN North Africa.
MATURE HEIGHT To 24m/80ft.
TRUNK To 30cm/12in in diameter, covered with rough old leaf scars; often seen damaged or distorted; produces suckers freely when allowed, but these are generally removed, leaving a solitary trunk.
LEAF Feather shaped, like *Phoenix canariensis*, but leaflets stiffer, coarser and fewer with a distinctive grey green coloration.
FLOWER STALK From among the leaf bases.
FRUIT The well-known date; many varieties have been developed.
SEED Long and narrow, grooved, with pointed ends.
CULTIVATION The date palm is easily grown from seed, which germinates well and readily, usually within a few weeks of sowing. Alternatively, it can be grown from suckers removed from the parent plant. *OUTDOORS* Although not as cold tolerant as *P. canariensis*, it is easily grown in warm temperate areas. The sexes are on separate trees. *INDOORS* It is just as suitable as *P. canariensis* for indoor growing, but its foliage is harder and less attractive.

PHOENIX ROEBELENII
PYGMY DATE PALM

A comparatively small-growing date palm, it is very popular for indoor use, forming a perfect miniature palm tree.
ORIGIN Laos, in South-East Asia.
MATURE HEIGHT To only about 3m/10ft.
TRUNK Slim, solitary, only about 7.5 or 10cm/3 or 4in in diameter; sometimes the old leaf bases project in a distinctive fashion, like pegs.
LEAF Feather shaped; the leaflets much softer than those of all the other phoenix palms, though the lower ones still form sharp spines.
FLOWER STALK From among the leaf bases.
FRUIT Small, about 12mm/½in long, brown when ripe.
SEED Typical date stone shape.
CULTIVATION The small seeds germinate readily, generally within six to eight weeks of sowing. *OUTDOORS* A perfect palm for the smaller garden, it grows in tropical, subtropical and warm temperate zones. *INDOORS* It is an equally wonderful palm for indoors, where it tolerates low light and abuse, but prefers bright indirect light. Sometimes a lack of iron can cause the leaves to turn yellow. It also looks good on the terrace in the warmer months.

PHOENIX RUPICOLA
CLIFF DATE PALM

Arguably the most attractive of all the date palms, it has a graceful habit and glossy leaflets, which are much finer than those of the other phoenix palms, with the exception of *P. roebelenii*.
ORIGIN India.
MATURE HEIGHT To 7.5m/25ft.
TRUNK Slim, solitary, with scars left by old leaves.
LEAF Feather shaped, and flat, with glossy leaflets; sometimes the leaves are twisted so they are perpendicular to the ground.
FLOWER STALK From among the leaf bases.
FRUIT 18mm/¾in long, dark red when ripe.
SEED 12mm/½in long, narrow, grooved along its length.
CULTIVATION The seeds germinate easily and readily. *OUTDOORS* This palm grows in a wide range of climates, from tropical to warm temperate. Lots of water in dry weather will be much appreciated and will help the palm to look its best. *INDOORS* It is not much used as a house plant, but there is no reason why it should not succeed.

Phoenix theophrastii
CRETAN DATE PALM

This recently-described palm is one of only two species native to Europe, the other being *Chamaerops humilis*, the Mediterranean fan palm. The Cretan date palm should be more widely grown, as it is a handsome plant, and should be moderately hardy to cold tolerant.
ORIGIN Crete, and the western edge of Turkey.
MATURE HEIGHT To about 6m/20ft.
TRUNK Clumping, slim, covered with old leaf scars.
LEAF Feather shaped, sometimes an attractive silvery grey green.
FLOWER STALK From among the leaf bases.
FRUIT 18mm/¾in long, dark brown when ripe.
SEED 12mm/½in long, shaped like other phoenix seeds, with a groove along the length.
CULTIVATION It is easily grown from seed, which germinates readily. *OUTDOORS* A palm for the temperate areas of the world, where it requires full sun, and permanent access to ground water. It should be moderately frost tolerant. *INDOORS* It has not been tried as a house plant, but should succeed in a brightly lit position.

Pigafetta filaris
WANGA PALM

A very fast-growing tropical palm, it seems to have discovered its own ecological niche in disturbed soil, often at the sides of new roads or where rainforest trees have been cut down. This would suggest that it needs bright light to succeed.
ORIGIN Confined to a few isolated islands in South-East Asia.
MATURE HEIGHT Tall, up to 45m/150ft.
TRUNK Sometimes over 30cm/12in in diameter, closely ringed.
LEAF Elegantly recurved feather leaf, the base of which is covered with light brown spines; these form horizontal narrow stripes in a very distinctive fashion.
FLOWER STALK From among the lower leaves.
FRUIT Small, no more than 12mm/½in long, covered with pretty scales, like snakeskin.
SEED Small and oval.
CULTIVATION The small seeds need to be planted immediately, as they lose their viability extremely quickly, possibly within days. *OUTDOORS* This is a beautiful palm for the tropical garden, but will probably not succeed elsewhere. Plant it in a sunny position, and never allow the plant to dry out. *INDOORS* It would be difficult to keep indoors, even in a humid glasshouse, but worth a try if enough light could be provided for the young seedling.

Pinanga coronata

One of a genus containing well over 100 species, it is commonly seen in forests and undergrowth of its native home.
ORIGIN Mainly confined to Malaysia, and some neighbouring countries.
MATURE HEIGHT To 4.5m/15ft.
TRUNK Multiple, clustered, slim and green, with prominent rings and a crownshaft.
LEAF A feather leaf, broad for its length.
FLOWER STALK From below the lowest leaves.
FRUIT Small, shiny and bright red; black when ripe.
SEED Small, pointed at one end.
CULTIVATION *Pinangas* mainly require tropical conditions, though some species show a certain tolerance to cold. *OUTDOORS* A shady protected spot in the humid tropics would suit this attractive palm best. Provide plenty of water in dry weather. *INDOORS* Pinangas show some promise as indoor plants if attention is paid to humidity and warmth, which should be gentle and constant. Young plants often have mottled leaves.

Pinanga kuhlii
IVORY CANE PALM

Another attractive *pinanga*, it has mottled leaves, especially as a young plant. Sometimes seen for sale as a house plant, it is commonly grown in the tropics, and can generally be seen in botanic gardens there.
ORIGIN Indonesia.
MATURE HEIGHT To 7.5m/25ft.
TRUNK Multiple, clumping, slim, elegant, green, ringed.
LEAF Feather shaped, with few, broad leaflets; these are often attractively mottled, especially in juvenile plants.
FLOWER STALK From below the crownshaft.
FRUIT 12mm/½in long, bright red when ripe.
SEED Oval.
CULTIVATION The ivory cane palm is easily grown from seed, which needs to be very fresh to germinate. *OUTDOORS* This species is rather more cold tolerant than many others in the genus, however it still requires at least warm temperate conditions to succeed. *INDOORS* It may be tried indoors – the beautiful mottled foliage of the young plants makes worthwhile any special efforts required to provide warmth and humidity.

PRITCHARDIA PACIFICA
FIJI FAN PALM

For many, this is the ultimate tropical palm, and the very essence of the tropics.
ORIGIN Fiji.
MATURE HEIGHT To 9m/30ft.
TRUNK Solitary, about 30cm/12in in diameter.
LEAF Beautiful, stiff, fan-shaped leaf, deeply pleated and light green in colour.
FLOWER STALK From among the leaves.
FRUIT 12mm/$\frac{1}{2}$in in diameter, black when ripe.
SEED Round, small.
CULTIVATION This palm is easily grown from seed, which germinates in a few weeks. *OUTDOORS* Tropical or subtropical conditions suit this palm best, together with an abundance of water in dry weather. They are often seen with yellow discoloration of the leaves, which may be a nutrient deficiency. *INDOORS* Not really suitable as a house plant, it may be grown for a few years in a humid glasshouse.

PTYCHOSPERMA ELEGANS
SOLITAIRE PALM

One of the most commonly seen of its genus, it has a solitary trunk.
ORIGIN North-eastern Australia.
MATURE HEIGHT To 9m/30ft.
TRUNK Slim, solitary, grey, ringed with old leaf scars; crownshaft.
LEAF Feather shaped, with fairly broad leaflets, the ends of which look as though they have been nibbled.
FLOWER STALK From below the crownshaft.
FRUIT Borne in large numbers, about 18mm/$\frac{3}{4}$in long, red when ripe.
SEED Distinctive, with grooves running along its length.
CULTIVATION The seeds germinate quickly and easily, usually within a few weeks of sowing, but need to be fresh for good results. *OUTDOORS* An attractive, small palm for the tropical and humid garden, it appreciates plenty of water in dry weather. *INDOORS* They are often seen in planting schemes in shopping malls and similar locations where, if bright light and enough humidity can be maintained, they do well.

PTYCHOSPERMA MACARTHURII
MACARTHUR PALM

A clumping ptychosperma, it is a common sight in botanic gardens throughout the tropics. The bright red fruits, freely borne, make it easy to identify.

ORIGIN North-East Australia.
MATURE HEIGHT To 9m/25ft.
TRUNK Multiple and clustering, slim, and ringed with old leaf scars; crownshaft.
LEAF Feather shaped, the fairly regular and broad leaflets having jagged ends.
FLOWER STALK From below the crownshaft.
FRUIT Bright red when ripe, about 18mm/¾in long.
SEED Grooved along its length, in typical ptychosperma fashion.
CULTIVATION Seeds that are fresh will sprout within a few weeks of planting. *OUTDOORS* A useful palm for the tropical garden, it occupies the minimum amount of space, but provides an attractive shape and colour. *INDOORS* It may certainly be tried indoors, but attention must be paid to levels of warmth and humidity.

RAPHIA FARINIFERA
RAFFIA PALM

This genus of palms has the longest leaves of any plants in the vegetable kingdom – up to 18m/60ft long. They were often used in the past for the production of raffia string, but this has lessened with the greater use of man-made materials.

ORIGIN Madagascar.
MATURE HEIGHT To 21m/70ft, much of this being taken up by the leaves, which grow on comparatively short trunks.
TRUNK Multiple; each trunk grows only to about 3m/10ft and 30cm/12in or more in diameter; the trunk dies after fruiting, but is replaced by others.
LEAF Among the longest in the plant kingdom; a massive feather-shaped leaf up to 18m/60ft long, held erect.
FLOWER STALK A massive structure that hangs down from the leaves.
FRUIT Large, up to 7.5cm/3in long, and covered with attractive scales.
SEED 4cm/1½in long, grooved and furrowed.
CULTIVATION The large seeds seem difficult to germinate, and would certainly have to be fresh for success. *OUTDOORS* Swampy ground in the humid tropics would suit this massive, water-loving palm admirably. Much space would be required to appreciate its size and beauty. *INDOORS* It is not known to be used indoors, where lack of humidity and light would undoubtedly be limiting factors.

RAVENEA RIVULARIS
MAJESTY PALM

An exciting "new" palm, it is becoming famous for its fast growth, and tolerance of cool conditions.
ORIGIN Madagascar.
MATURE HEIGHT To 12m/40ft.
TRUNK 30cm/12in or more in diameter.
LEAF An elegant feather-shaped leaf, which clasps the trunk in a distinctive manner.
FLOWER STALK From among the leaves.
FRUIT 12mm/$\frac{1}{2}$in in diameter, round.
SEED Small, round.
CULTIVATION The small seeds germinate easily, but only if absolutely fresh, as they lose their viability very quickly. *OUTDOORS* A beautiful palm for tropics, sub-tropics and warm temperate areas, it grows extremely quickly. Much water appreciated in dry weather. *INDOORS* This palm, which has only recently been brought into cultivation, seems to thrive indoors, tolerating low light, and growing well, even in comparatively cool conditions.

REINHARDTIA GRACILIS
WINDOW PALM

A tiny, dainty and beautiful palm, it is much in demand as a house plant. The common name refers to the holes, or "windows" in the leaves.
ORIGIN Central America.
MATURE HEIGHT To only 1.2 or 1.5m/4 or 5ft.
TRUNK Mutliple, very thin, only about 2.5cm/1in in diameter.
LEAF A feather leaf, but with only a few broad leaflets, often with small holes or "windows" at their base.
FLOWER STALK From among the leaves.
FRUIT Small, 12mm/$\frac{1}{2}$in in circumference, and black when ripe.
SEED Small, round and wrinkled.
CULTIVATION The small seeds germinate quite easily if fresh. *OUTDOORS* A position in the tropical garden that is protected from both sun and wind would suit these small palms best, together with an abundance of water in dry weather. *INDOORS* These splendid house plants are difficult to grow, but worth any special effort. Protect them from direct light, and pay attention to the humidity.

RHAPIDOPHYLLUM HYSTRIX
NEEDLE PALM

Certainly the most cold-tolerant palm known, it will survive incredibly low temperatures, but requires summer heat to grow well.
ORIGIN South-eastern USA.
MATURE HEIGHT To 2.1 or 2.4m/7 or 8ft only, and as wide.
TRUNK The short trunk may be underground, or grow to a few feet above ground. It suckers very freely and unless trimmed the plant grows into a dense, impenetrable bush. The trunks are covered with vertical, sharp, black spines, up to 10cm/4in long, among which the seeds drop, often germinating there and then dying for lack of water and nutrients.
LEAF Fan shaped, dark glossy green above, paler beneath.
FLOWER STALK Almost lost among the leaf bases and spines.
FRUIT 18mm/¾in long, ovoid in shape.
SEED 12mm/½in long, grooved down one side.
CULTIVATION The seeds are difficult to obtain and erratic to germinate. *OUTDOORS* This palm grows best in warm temperate areas with good hot summers, and can be planted either in shade or full sun. In cooler areas they grow slowly, and require a sunny position. This is one of the few truly hardy palms. *INDOORS* It is not known to have been tried indoors.

RHAPIS EXCELSA
LADY PALM

This is possibly the perfect indoor palm, tolerating low light levels, and growing slowly to an impressive size over a number of years.
ORIGIN Southern China.
MATURE HEIGHT To 3m/10ft.
TRUNK Multiple, very slim, covered in dark woven fibres; forms a large clump or bush, with leaves all the way down to the ground.
LEAF Fan shaped, deeply cut, dark glossy green in colour, the ends of the leaflets are squared off and jagged.
FLOWER STALK From among the leaf bases, towards the top of the plant.
FRUIT Small, 12mm/½in in diameter.
SEED Small and round.
CULTIVATION The small seeds are easy to germinate, but the young seedlings grow extremely slowly. Plants may also be grown from suckers from a parent plant. *OUTDOORS* The lady palm will grow in sun or shade, and in tropical, subtropical or warm temperate areas. A very adaptable palm, it shows some tolerance to cold. *INDOORS* Unsurpassed as a house palm, it is extremely tolerant of low light and dry air, though the plants should never be allowed to dry out. Variegated specimens are sometimes available. Possibly the only drawback is their high price, which is related to the plants' slow growth.

RHAPIS HUMILIS
SLENDER LADY PALM

The slender lady palm is similar in general appearance to the foregoing. All plants in cultivation are grown from suckers, as female plants are not known. It is not often seen for sale; plants bought as *R. humilis* often turn out to be a third species, *R. subtilis,* which is much more tropical.
ORIGIN Not known for certain, but likely to be China.
MATURE HEIGHT To 3.6m/12ft.
TRUNK Slim, multiple, again covered in woven dark fibres.
LEAF Generally similar to those of *R. excelsa,* but the leaflet tips are pointed, instead of being squared off; the leaflets are also narrower, and more numerous.
FLOWER STALK Male only, from among the leaf bases, towards the top of the plants.
FRUIT Not known to exist; seeds offered as *R. humilis* are almost certain to be another species of rhapis, or, worse, another species of palm.
SEED See above.
CULTIVATION This species must be propagated vegetatively, that is, from suckers. *OUTDOORS* Plants will grow in a wide range of climates and conditions, in shade or sun, though they certainly look more refreshed in shade. *INDOORS* An excellent indoor species, it will put up with low light and general abuse. Do not, however, allow the soil to dry out.

RHOPALOSTYLIS SAPIDA
NIKAU OR SHAVING-BRUSH PALM

Easily recognizable by its swollen, almost round crownshaft, this species is native to New Zealand.
ORIGIN New Zealand.
MATURE HEIGHT To 7.5m/25ft.
TRUNK Solitary, about 20 or 22.5cm/8 or 9in in diameter, with a prominent crownshaft, which, together with the erect leaves, gives it its common name of shaving-brush palm.
LEAF Feather shaped, leaflets pointed, with prominent veins.
FLOWER STALK From below the crownshaft.
FRUIT 18mm/³⁄₄in in diameter, red when ripe.
SEED 12mm/¹⁄₂in in diameter, one side carries a scar.
CULTIVATION The seeds take two or three months to germinate and seedling growth is quite slow. *OUTDOORS* The nikau prefers a cool, shady, moist location, definitely out of direct sunlight. Rich soil and an abundance of water will result in quite steady growth, even in temperate areas. However, *R. sapida* is only cold tolerant down to $-4°C/24°F$, and it must be protected if colder weather threatens. It is one of the few hardy feather palms. *INDOORS* Not known to be used as a house plant, it shows some promise, however, in view of its preference for low light.

ROYSTONEA ELATA
FLORIDA ROYAL PALM

One of several species much planted as ornamentals in tropical countries, it is easily recognized by the huge, towering, almost white trunks and glossy green crownshafts.
ORIGIN Florida, USA.
MATURE HEIGHT To 24m/80ft.
TRUNK Solitary, thick, pale grey to white, with a prominent green crownshaft.
LEAF Plumose (like a bottle brush), and with a feather-shaped leaf.
FLOWER STALK From below the crownshaft, erect.
FRUIT Small and round, perhaps 12mm/$\frac{1}{2}$in in diameter.
SEED Small and round; somehow it seems curious that such a massive tree could grow from such a small seed.
CULTIVATION The seeds germinate easily and rapidly. *OUTDOORS* Consider long and hard before deciding where to plant this large and beautiful tropical tree, as it will certainly dominate the landscape for many years to come. Often seen in avenues in the tropics, they make remarkably even growth. *INDOORS* Although not much tried indoors, it would probably be possible to grow it for a few years, if attention were paid to humidity and light.

ROYSTONEA REGIA
CUBAN ROYAL PALM

This is closely related to the foregoing, and usually distinguishable by the trunk. However, since individuals can be so variable, this is not a reliable means of identification.
ORIGIN Cuba.
MATURE HEIGHT To 21m/70ft, less than *R. elata*.
TRUNK Massive, pale grey or whitish, often bulging at the base and again in the middle section; prominent green crownshaft.
LEAF Feather shaped, leaflets at different angles.
FLOWER STALK From below the crownshaft, erect.
FRUIT Small, 12mm/$\frac{1}{2}$in in diameter.
SEED Small, round and insignificant.
CULTIVATION This palm is easily grown from seed, which germinates readily. *OUTDOORS* A tropical palm, it requires full sun and plenty of water in dry weather. *INDOORS* This is not used as a house plant, but it would be possible to use it this way for a few years.

PALM IDENTIFIER

Sabal minor
BLUE OR DWARF PALMETTO PALM

A fairly low-growing, trunkless *sabal*, it is extremely cold-hardy, though it needs summer heat to grow well.
ORIGIN South-eastern USA.
MATURE HEIGHT To 3.6m/12ft.
TRUNK Trunkless, or with an underground stem, sometimes rising a few feet above ground.
LEAF Very stiff, blue green, fan-shaped leaf, which is costapalmate (the leaf stem continues into the leaf).
FLOWER STALK From among the leaves and rising to perhaps twice the height of the plant.
FRUIT Small, 12mm/½in in circumference, black when ripe.
SEED Small, round, slightly flattened, and a glossy dark red brown.
CULTIVATION This palm is easily grown from seed, which germinates quickly. *OUTDOORS* Requiring full sun, in tropical to temperate zones, this palm needs much heat to succeed, although it is extremely hardy to cold, being one of the most cold-hardy palms, in fact. It prefers swampy ground, and is slow growing. *INDOORS* It may be grown indoors, but requires very bright light; lack of humidity is not, however, a problem.

Sabal palmetto
PALMETTO PALM

A tall-growing *sabal*, this is Florida's state tree.
ORIGIN South-eastern USA.
MATURE HEIGHT To 24m/80ft.
TRUNK Solitary, up to 45cm/18in in diameter, usually less; older part of the trunk smooth, but above that, it is covered with old leaf bases which are split into two in a distinctive fashion.
LEAF Stiff, green, costapalmate.
FLOWER STALK From among the leaf bases.
FRUIT Small, 12mm/½in in diameter, black when ripe.
SEED Small, round and slightly flattened.
CULTIVATION Easily germinated, the small seeds sprout in a few weeks. *OUTDOORS* This is an interesting palm for the tropics and sub-tropics, where it grows quickly. The old leaves hang down and should be trimmed back for a neat appearance. *INDOORS* Not much used as a house plant, it would certainly be possible to keep this palm in a high-light situation.

SERENOA REPENS
SAW PALMETTO

A small palm, it is native to Florida and the surrounding areas, where it covers huge areas of land. Silver and blue forms are sometimes seen.
ORIGIN South-eastern USA.
MATURE HEIGHT To 2.4 or 2.7m/8 or 9ft, usually much less.
TRUNK Usually underground, or at best, only a few feet tall; clump forming.
LEAF Stiff, small, fan shaped, silver, blue or green.
FLOWER STALK From among the leaves.
FRUIT 18mm/¾in long, oval, black when ripe.
SEED 12mm/½in long.
CULTIVATION The seeds germinate easily, though this may take several weeks. Plants may also be reproduced from suckers. *OUTDOORS* Full sun is best, together with adequate moisture, and a tropical to temperate climate. This species shows some tolerance of cold. *INDOORS* Although it is not known as a house plant, it might be worth any special effort to grow this attractive small palm. Dry air is unlikely to be a problem, but insufficient light might cause difficulties.

SYAGRUS ROMANZOFFIANA
QUEEN PALM

Well known and popular, it was until recently known as *Arecastrum romanzoffianum*, and prior to that *Cocos plumosa*, by which name it is still found for sale in nurseries.
ORIGIN Brazil.
MATURE HEIGHT To 18m/60ft.
TRUNK Solitary, and ringed with old leaf bases; no crownshaft.
LEAF Plumose, that is, with the leaflets radiating at different angles.
FLOWER STALK From among the leaf bases.
FRUIT To 2.5cm/1in long, yellow when ripe.
SEED 18mm/¾in long, covered in fibres.
CULTIVATION Easily germinated from seed, and the first simple leaves can be up to 90cm/3ft or more long. *OUTDOORS* It will grow in a wide range of climates, from tropical to temperate, and appreciates much water and fertilizer. It grows very fast, and shows some tolerance to cold. *INDOORS* Indoor cultivation is possible, given sufficient light levels.

TRACHYCARPUS FORTUNEI

The common name "Chusan palm" derives from the fact that it was on Chusan Island – or Chou-Shan or Zhoushan as it's now known – that Robert Fortune, the famous 19th-century plant hunter, first saw the palm that was to bear his name. However, the trees he saw were more than likely cultivated specimens. Zhoushan Island is in the East China Sea, off Hangzhou (Hangchow), south of Shanghai, and at one time it was to have been the main British settlement in the area. However, the final choice was another tiny island – Hong Kong – and the rest is history.

TRACHYCARPUS FORTUNEI
CHUSAN PALM

This is perhaps the most popular palm for cooler climates, where it grows well with the minimum of care and attention, and is extremely hardy to cold, frost and snow. An attractive form called *T. wagnerianus* has much smaller, stiffer leaves, particularly apparent in young plants, but is certainly not a distinct species. In the United States, this form is often misnamed *T. takil*.
ORIGIN China; *Trachycarpus takil*, probably only another form, comes from the western Indian Himalayas.
MATURE HEIGHT To 12m/40ft.
TRUNK Slim, solitary, covered with old leaf bases, and brown fibrous matted hairy fibres; if not trimmed, the old leaves hang down in the manner of Washingtonia. In some countries, the fibres are stripped as a matter of course, leaving a bare trunk, so the hairy trunk should not be considered a reliable identifying feature.
LEAF Fan shaped, 1.2m/4ft across, irregularly divided.
FLOWER STALK From among the lower leaves, yellow.
FRUIT Kidney shaped, about 12mm/½in long, a blue black when ripe, with a white bloom.
SEED Kidney shaped.
CULTIVATION The seeds germinate easily within a few weeks of sowing. *OUTDOORS* This is a plant for temperate to warm temperate zones, but unhappy in the tropics. It prefers a heavy rich clay soil, and hates both wind, which damages the leaves, and waterlogged soil. It is very cold hardy. *INDOORS* It may be grown as a house plant for a few years, but is much happier as a tub plant on the terrace, or in the ground.

THRINAX FLORIDANA
FLORIDA THATCH PALM

This is one of a number of species occurring in the West Indies, Central America and Florida.
ORIGIN Florida Keys.
MATURE HEIGHT To 9m/30ft.
TRUNK Slim, solitary, and lacking a crownshaft.
LEAF Fan shaped, or sometimes forming almost a complete circle; the leaf segments are cut to about half the depth of the leaf.
FLOWER STALK From among the leaf bases.
FRUIT Small and round, perhaps 12mm/½in in diameter.
SEED 6mm/¼in in diameter.
CULTIVATION The small seeds germinate easily and readily.
OUTDOORS A position in full sun would suit these drought-tolerant palms best. *INDOORS* It is not known to be used as an indoor plant.

TRACHYCARPUS MARTIANUS

Quite different from *T. fortunei*, this elegant species has a naturally bare trunk, and differs in leaf and seed details.
ORIGIN Eastern Himalayas in northern India, southern Burma, and Assam.
MATURE HEIGHT To 12m/40ft.
TRUNK Slim, solitary, usually bare except for the area immediately below the crown.
LEAF Fan shaped, regularly divided to about half way, glossy, and mid-green in colour.
FLOWER STALK From among the leaf bases; flowers are white, as opposed to yellow.
FRUIT Oval in shape, 12mm/½in long.
SEED Oval, grooved down one side like a date seed.
CULTIVATION The seeds germinate readily within two to three months of sowing. The young seedlings seem prone to all manner of pests and should be given preventative treatment. *OUTDOORS* Warm temperate to temperate conditions would seem best for this beautiful but rarely grown palm. It is less cold hardy than its cousin, and more effort should be made to introduce it to botanic as well as private gardens. *INDOORS* This species seems to be vulnerable to attack by every known insect pest. As with seedlings, treat as a preventative rather than as a cure.

TRACHYCARPUS NANUS

The third and last species in the *Trachycarpus* genus, this one does not grow a trunk. Though it is recorded as being locally common in its home country, it has never been brought into cultivation and has only recently even been photographed.
ORIGIN South-western China.
MATURE HEIGHT To perhaps 1.2m/4ft.
TRUNK Either trunkless, or with an underground stem.
LEAF Fan shaped and stiffly held.
FLOWER STALK From among the leaf bases, erect.
FRUIT Apparently similar to *T. fortunei*, that is, 12mm/½in long, kidney shaped, blue black when ripe, with a white bloom.
SEED Kidney shaped.
CULTIVATION Nothing is known of the germination or cultural requirements of this palm.

TRITHRINAX ACANTHACOMA
SPINY FIBRE PALM

The unattractive common name describes a most attractive palm, which grows in a wide range of climates, and is gradually becoming more popular, the spines on the trunk being a possible deterrent to its use. It is easily mistaken for *Trachycarpus fortunei* at a distance.
ORIGIN Brazil.
MATURE HEIGHT To 6m/20ft.
TRUNK Solitary, covered with old leaf bases and an intricate pattern of fibres and sharp spines, somewhat dangerous to the touch.
LEAF Fan shaped, green, rather stiff in appearance, with spines at the leaf tips.
FLOWER STALK From among the leaves.
FRUIT 2.5cm/1in in diameter, round, white to pale green when ripe, hanging in large clusters, like grapes.
SEED Round, 12mm/½in in diameter.
CULTIVATION The seeds germinate in about eight to ten weeks.
OUTDOORS This is an interesting palm for warm temperate to temperate zones, and it shows some tolerance to cold. It is slow growing, especially in the early stages. *INDOORS* It may be grown as a young plant for a few years, bright light being the main requirement.

TRITHRINAX CAMPESTRIS

An incredibly beautiful, low-growing palm, with multiple stems and the stiffest leaves of any palm. The fact that it is very slow growing probably accounts for its rarity, even in botanic collections.
ORIGIN Argentina.
MATURE HEIGHT To 1.8m/6ft, perhaps more.
TRUNK Forms a small clump, with perhaps three or four trunks, about 22.5 or 25cm/9 or 10in in diameter, each covered in the most intricate woven fibres and spines, which are incredibly stiff and hard.
LEAF Fan shaped, about 30–45cm/12–18in long, incredibly stiff and tipped with sharp spines; pale blue, almost white, in colour.
FLOWER STALK From among the leaves.
FRUIT Round, 18mm/¾in in diameter.
SEED 12mm/½in in diameter.
CULTIVATION The small seeds are not easy to germinate, but it is well worth persevering in order to grow this fabulous palm. *OUTDOORS* Because it is so stiff and spiny, it should be planted well away from paths and walkways. Choose a position in full sun, in free-draining soil. Hot, dry and bright conditions are ideal for this palm. *INDOORS* It would probably do very well in a bright conservatory.

VEITCHIA MERRILLII
CHRISTMAS PALM

Often thought to be a miniature royal palm, *Veitchia* is becoming more popular in cultivation, and is often seen in shopping centres and office plantings, as well as for street planting in Florida.
ORIGIN Philippines.
MATURE HEIGHT To 6m/20ft.
TRUNK Solitary, pale, smooth, with indistinct rings; green crownshaft, usually swollen at the base.
LEAF Feather shaped and recurved, with the leaflets pointing upwards forming a valley shape; additionally, each leaflet is usually twisted in on itself.
FLOWER STALK From below the crownshaft.
FRUIT About 2.5cm/1in, bright red when ripe and said to resemble Christmas decorations, as they fruit in December.
SEED 12mm/½in in circumference.
CULTIVATION Easily grown from seed which germinates, if fresh, within a few weeks of sowing. *OUTDOORS* Tropical and subtropical conditions suit these small palms best, together with an abundance of water. It is quite fast growing. *INDOORS* This is an attractive plant for interior use, but provide good light and allow the soil to dry out at the surface between thorough waterings.

Verschaffeltia splendida

A beautiful simple-leaved palm, requiring tropical conditions, or a hot and humid glasshouse.
ORIGIN Seychelles Islands.
MATURE HEIGHT To 15m/50ft, but usually much less.
TRUNK Solitary, dark brown, with spines on younger plants; on older trees the trunks are smooth and spineless; stilt roots soon develop, which lift the tree clear of the ground.
LEAF In sheltered locations, the leaves are simple and entire; where it is windy, the leaf usually splits, resulting in a feather shape.
FLOWER STALK From among the leaves.
FRUIT Round, 2.5cm/1in in diameter.
SEED 18mm/³⁄₄in in diameter, ridged and grooved in an unmistakable fashion; very hard.
CULTIVATION The attractive seeds germinate easily if fresh. *OUTDOORS* For best results, this palm should be planted where it is totally sheltered from wind, in a tropical location. Plenty of water is appreciated. *INDOORS* This is only likely to succeed in a tropical glasshouse, as its demand for humidity is paramount.

Wallichia densiflora

A small clustering palm from the Himalayas, it is fairly hardy to cold, and should be much more widely grown.
ORIGIN The low Himalayas of north India and Assam.
MATURE HEIGHT To 3m/10ft, possibly more.
TRUNK Very short, or non-existent; clump forming.
LEAF Reminiscent of the fish-tail palms, with jagged or toothed tips and edges; green above, silvery beneath.
FLOWER STALK From among the leaves.
FRUIT 12mm/¹⁄₂in in diameter, oval.
SEED Small, round.
CULTIVATION The small seeds are difficult and erratic to germinate. *OUTDOORS* This will grow in zones ranging from temperate to warm temperate, but is not suitable for the tropics. It will tolerate several degrees of frost, but needs rich soil. *INDOORS* Not known to be grown indoors, it is, however, probably suitable for conservatory use.

WALLICHIA DISTICHA
WALLICH'S PALM

Unfortunately extremely rare in cultivation, this is one of the few truly two-dimensional trees, the leaves growing in one plane, giving a flat appearance from the side, in the manner of the Traveller's palm, *Ravanela madagascariensis*.

ORIGIN North-East India, Sikkim.
MATURE HEIGHT To 6m/20ft.
TRUNK Solitary, and covered in old leaf bases and fibres.
LEAF The leaves grow in two ranks, erect; leaflets in two planes thus somewhat plumose; an unmistakable formation.
FLOWER STALK From among the leaf bases; flowering is monocarpic, that is, when flowering and fruiting is finished, the tree dies.
FRUIT 18mm/¾in in circumference, dark red when ripe.
SEED 12mm/½in in diameter, round.
CULTIVATION The seeds are slow and erratic to germinate. *OUTDOORS* Tropical conditions are preferred, with lots of water in dry weather and full sun. *INDOORS* This is not known as an indoor plant.

WASHINGTONIA FILIFERA
CALIFORNIAN COTTON PALM

Very commonly planted in many parts of the world, its popularity is largely due to its fast growth, and consequent cheapness. Established plants show some resistance to cold.

ORIGIN South-West USA.
MATURE HEIGHT To 18m/60ft.
TRUNK Solitary, up to 75cm/2½ft or more thick, sometimes covered with a thick layer of old leaves which may extend down to the ground, though this is often removed to expose the trunk, which is smooth with vertical fissures.
LEAF Fan shaped, with thread-like fibres between the leaflets.
FLOWER STALK From among the leaves, long and arching out beyond the leaves. This feature distinguishes it from *Livistona australis*, with which it might otherwise be confused.
FRUIT Small, round.
SEED Small, round, dark glossy red.
CULTIVATION The small seeds germinate as easily as grass and are said to have a very long viability, perhaps several years. *OUTDOORS* Temperate to tropical climates suit this adaptable palm, which moves successfully at almost any age. They are drought resistant and grow best in full sun. *INDOORS* An easy and interesting indoor plant, it requires bright indirect light to flourish.

WASHINGTONIA ROBUSTA
SKYDUSTER

Taller and thinner than the foregoing, this well-named palm grows quickly to an impressive height, and is the palm in the background of all those television crime series shot in Los Angeles.
ORIGIN North Mexico.
MATURE HEIGHT To 30m/100ft.
TRUNK Much thinner and taller than *W. filifera*, but equally likely to be clothed with a thick layer of dead leaves.
LEAF Fan shaped, perhaps smaller than the foregoing.
FLOWER STALK From among the leaf bases, and longer than the leaves, an important distinguishing feature.
FRUIT Small, round.
SEED Small, round, dark red, glossy.
CULTIVATION The seeds germinate rapidly, within a few weeks, and may be stored for long periods. The desert origin of the Washingtonias can be thanked for this. *OUTDOORS* Temperate to tropical areas are home to this fast-growing palm, where it thrives in full sun. Drought tolerant, it also has the advantage of moving easily at any age. *INDOORS* Another good interior plant, it thrives in bright light, and makes a super conservatory plant for cool climates.

WODYETIA BIFURCATA
FOX-TAIL PALM

This is a beautiful and fast-growing Australian palm. *Bifurcata* refers to the fibres on the seeds, which fork in a distinctive fashion.
ORIGIN North-East Australia.
MATURE HEIGHT To 12m/40ft.
TRUNK Solitary, distinctly ringed, about 22.5cm/9in thick, with crownshaft.
LEAF Plumose, that is, with the leaflets radiating out from the leaf stalk, giving a bottle brush, or fox-tail appearance; leaflets fine and narrow.
FLOWER STALK From below the crownshaft.
FRUIT 5cm/2in long, oval, red when ripe.
SEED 4cm/1½in long, with unique forking fibres.
CULTIVATION The large seeds germinate within two or three months, and subsequent growth is very fast in hot conditions. *OUTDOORS* This drought-tolerant palm grows well in dry soils, but improves markedly with an abundance of water. *INDOORS* Not known to be tried indoors, it would probably be successful if light levels were high enough.

INDEX

A
Acoelorrhaphe wrightii 15
African date palm 60
Aiphanes erosa 15
Alexander palm 16
Andean wax palm 27, 28
Archontophoenix alexandrae 16
Archontophoenix cunninghamiana 16
Areca catechii 17
Areca ipot 17
Areca palm 33
Areca triandra 18
Areca vestiaria 18
Arecastrum romanzoffianum 72
Arenga engleri 19
Arenga pinnata 19
Arenga undulatifolia 20
Assai palm 41
Atherton palm 48
Australian fan palm 52
axil 12

B
Bactris gasipaes 20
Bailey's copernica palm 36
bamboo palm 38
Bangalow palm 16
Bertam 41
Betel nut palm 17
bi-pinnate 12
Bismarck palm 21
Bismarckia nobilis 21
Black palm 56
Blue Latin palm 49
Blue or dwarf palmetto palm 71
Borassus flabellifer 22
Borrassodendron machadonis 21
Bottle palm 45
Brahea armata 23
Brahea edulis 23
Butia capitata 24
Butia palm 24
Butterfly palm 33

C
cabbage 12
Californian cotton palm 78
Canary island date palm 60
Calamus 25
Calamus australis 25
Caryota mitis 24
Caryota no 26
Caryota obtusa 26
Caryota urens 27
Ceroxylon alpinum 27
Ceroxylon andicola 27
Ceroxylon quindiuense 28
Chamaerops humilis 28
Chameadorea elegans 29
Chameadorea erumpens 30
Chameadorea geonomaeformis 30
Chameadorea klotzschiana 31
Chameadorea metallica 31
Chameadorea stolonifera 32
Chilean wine palm 47
Chinese fan palm 52
Christmas palm 76
Chuniophoenix hainanensis 32
Chusan palm 73
Chrysalidocarpus lutescens 33
Chrysalidocarpus madogascariensis 33
cleaning leaves 9
Cliff date palm 62
Coccothrinax argentea 34
Coccothrinax crinita 34
Coco-de-mer 53
Coconut palm 35
Cocos nucifera 35
Cocos plumosa 72
Copernica baileyana 35
Copernica macroglossa 36
Corypha elata 37
Corypha umbraculifera 37
costapalmate 12
Cretan date palm 63
crownshaft 12
Cuban belly palm 42
Cuban petticoat palm 36

Cuban petticoat palm 36
Cuban royal palm 70
Cyrtostachys renda 38

D
Daemonorops angustifolia 38
Date palm 61
Deckenia nobilis 39
Dictyosperma album 39
Double coconut 53
Doum palm 46

E
Elaeis guineensis 40
Eugeissona tristis 41
European Palm Society 7
Euterpe edulis 41

F
Fiji fan palm 65
Fish-tail palm 24, 26
Florida royal palm 70
Florida silver palm 34
Florida thatch palm 74
Footstool palm 53
Fountain palm 52
Fox-tail palm 79

G
Gastrococos crispa 42
glossary 12
Golden cane palm 33
Guadaloupe palm 23
Guihayaia argyrata 42

H
hastula 12
Hedescepe canterburyana 43
Howea belmoreana 43
Howea forsteriana 44
Hurricane palm 39
Hydraistele microspadix 44
Hyophorbe lagenicaulis 45
Hyophorbe verschaffeltii 45
Hyphaene dichotoma 46

I
indoor palms 8–10
  feed 9
  humidity 9
  light 8
  temperature 8
  water 9
International Palm Society 7
Ivory cane palm 64

J
Jelly palm 24
Johannestejsmannia altifrons 46
Jubaea chilensis 47
Jubaeaopsis caffra 48

K
Kentia palm 44
King palm 16

L
Laccospadix australasica 48
Lady palm 68
Latania loddigessii 49
Latania lontaroides 49
Latania verschaffeltii 50
Lawyer's cane 25
Licuala grandis 50
Licuala orbicularis 51
Licuala spinosa 51
Livistona australis 51
Livistona chinensis 52
Livistona rotundifolia 53
Lodoicea maldivica 53
Lytocaryum weddellianum 54

M
Macarthur palm 66
Macaw palm 15
Majesty palm 67
Mazari palm 55
Mediterranean fan palm 28
Metroxylon sagu 54
Mexican blue palm 23
Microcoeleum weddellianum 54
Miniature coconut palm 54

N
Nannorrhops ritchiana 55
Needle palm 68
Neodypsis decaryi 55
Nibung palm 57
Nikau or shaving-brush palm 69
Nipah palm 56
Normanbya normanbyi 56
Nypa fruticans 56

O
Oil palm 40
Oncosperma horridum 57
Oncosperma tigillarum 57
Oraniopsis appendiculata 58
outdoor palms 11–12
  fertilizing 11
  maintenance 12
  planting out 11
  roots 11
  watering 11, 12
  weight 11

P
palmate 12
Palmetto palm 71
Palmiste 39
palms, main varieties of 10
Palmyra palm 22

Parajubaea cocoides 58
Parlour palm 29
Paurotis wrightii 15
Peach palm 20
Pelagodoxa henryana 59
petiole 12
Phoenicophorium borsigianum 59
Phoenix canariensis 60
Phoenix dactylifera 61
Phoenix reclinata 60
Phoenix roebelenii 62
Phoenix rupicola 62
Phoenix theophrastii 63
Pigafetta filaris 63
Pinanga kuhlii 64
pinnate 12
Pondoland palm 48
Princess palm 39
Pritchardia pacifica 65
Ptychosperma elegans 65
Ptychosperma macarthurii 66
Pygmy date palm 62

Q
Queen palm 72

R
Raffia palm 66
Rajah palm 38
Raphia farinifera 66
Ravenea rivularis 67
Red Latan palm 49
Reed palm 32
Reinhardtia gracilis 67
Rhapidophyllum hystrix 68
Rhapis excelsa 68
Rhapis humilis 69
Rhopalostylis sapida 69
Roystonea elata 70
Roystonea regia 70
Ruffled fan palm 50

S
Sabal minor 71
Sabal palmetto 71
Sago palm 54
Saw palmetto 72
Sealing wax palm 38
Senegal date palm 60
Sentry palm 43
Serenoa repens 72
Silver saw palmetto 15
Skyduster 79
Slender lady palm 69
Solitaire palm 65
Spindle palm 45
Spiny fibre palm 75
Sugar palm 19
Syagrus romanzoffiana 72
symbols, key to 13

T
Talipot palm 37
Thrinax floridana 74
Trachycarpus fortunei 73
Trachycarpus martianus 74
Trachycarpus nanus 75
Trachycarpus takil 73
Trachycarpus wagnerianus 73
Triangle palm 55
Trithrinax acanthocoma 75
Trithrinax campestris 76

U
Umbrella palm 43

V
Veitchia merrillii 76
Verschaffeltia splendida 77

W
Wallichia densiflora 77
Wallichia disticha 78
Wallich's palm 78
Wanga palm 63
Washingtonia filifera 78
Washingtonia robusta 79
Window palm 67
Wine or jaggery palm 27
Wodyetia bifurcata 79

Y
Yellow Latin palm 50

PICTURE CREDITS

t = top   b = bottom

All the photographs featured in this book were taken by Martin Gibbons of the Palm Centre, except for the following:

Matthew Baldwin: p43(t), 77(b). Brad Carter: p69(b). Jacquez Deleuze: pp6, 16(b), 26(t), 56(b), 78(t). Bill Dickenson: p43(b). Inge Hoffmann: pp19(b), 37(t), 41(t and b), 72(t). Tony King: pp23(b), 24(t), 34(b), 36(t and b), 42(t), 47, 52(t and b), 68(t), 72(t). David Mclean: p30(t). Sam Mitchell: pp18(b), 27(b), 48(c), 54(t), 58(b). D. S. Neave: p37(b). Parks Department, Durban, South Africa: p48(t). Royal Botanic Gardens, Kew: pp34(t), 74(t). Rudolph Spanner: p75(t). Tobias Spanner: pp32(b), 59(t). Mick Turland: p63(t).